Find your Hedgehog and Stop Working

The Cornerstone to Building Your Business

Socrate Exantus

Cassandra Exantus

Find your Hedgehog and Stop Working

The Cornerstone to Building Your Business

Copyright © 2018 Socrate Exantus and Cassandra Exantus

All rights reserved.

—Disclaimer—

This publication is designed to provide accurate and authoritative information regarding the subject matter contained within. It should be understood that the author and publisher are not engaged in rendering legal, accounting, or other financial services through this medium. The author and publisher shall not be liable for your misuse of this material and shall have neither liability nor responsibility to anyone with respect to any loss or damage caused, or alleged to be caused, directly or indirectly by the information contained in this book.
The author and/or publisher do not guarantee that anyone following these strategies, suggestions, tips, ideas or techniques will become successful. If legal advice or other expert assistance is required, the services of a competent professional should be sought.

All rights reserved. No portion of this book may be reproduced mechanically, electronically, or by any other means, including photocopying, without written permission from the author. It is illegal to copy the book, post it to a website, or distribute it by any other means without permission from the author.

ISBN-13:978-1-946203-39-7

Author Contact Info
Socrate and Cassandra Exantus
(407) 349-4775
Socrate@GoCriticalPath.com
Cassandra@GoCriticalPath.com

www.ExpertPress.net

ACKNOWLEDGMENTS

This book has been in the making for nearly two decades. It's no surprise that some of the stories in this book date back to the late 1990s. As such, there are so many people to thank for their contribution to both Cassandra's and my professional growth. My professional career started at Sprint while I was still a college student. I want to thank everyone who coached and mentored me at Sprint and saw in me things that I had not yet seen in myself. There are too many to thank individually, but there were a few leaders who impacted me tremendously, namely my longtime mentor Monty Pollard.

I'd also like to acknowledge the trainers at the Sprint Training Department in Orlando, Florida; Bristol, Virginia; Kansas City, Kansas, and the amazing Loyalty Marketing Group (BG – RR) in Maitland, Florida, and lastly, the Business Inside Sales Organization (BISO). These friendships have lasted well beyond my leaving Sprint in 2009. For the last eight years, I have had the honor to lead the most incredible group of people in the business. Over the years, we have had at least six dozen people who have worked or currently work with us as business owners. However, there are some who are a part of the original five, without whom we do not know where our business would be. They are Sarah Rodgers, Reshard Battle, Calley Dittmer, Paula Givler, and Yarmmys Vargas. We thank you.

From a personal perspective, the culture of the family I was raised in led to my competitive spirit. My parents left everything they owned to start over in this country. That act alone taught my siblings and me that we could do and accomplish anything.

Thank you to all my brothers who both inspired me and challenged me to work hard, especially my oldest brother and mentor, William Exantus. Thank you for setting the bar for greatness.

To my love, best friend, and partner, Cassandra. You are the most amazingly talented and supportive person I know. This book would not have been possible without your belief, support, and co-authorship.

To my children Arylan and Socrate: I cried when I learned that Cassandra was pregnant with you, Arylan, because I wanted to the best father I could be. That thought was both exciting and intimidating. Thank you for teaching me how to be a father to an incredible little lady. To my namesake, Socrate Aurelius Exantus, thank you for showing me that even though I'm a man, I have to learn to be a father to a little boy. You seldom do what we want you to do, but you challenge us not to assume that parenting is a cakewalk.

We also want to thank each of our brothers for their contribution to who we are today: Herve Etienne, Reginal Etienne, William Exantus, Abel Exantus, Ricot Exantus, Jocelyn Exantus, Reginald Fils-Aime, Jean Exantus, Nixon Exantus, Jouvens Exantus, and Roody Exantus

From Cassandra:

Mom and Dad, thank you for your sacrifice, support, and love. To my brothers, you've enriched my life greatly. To the many hands that helped me along the way professionally and personally, I thank you dearly. To my closest family and friends (too many to name), thank you for always being in my corner. To my lovely daughter Arylan, I've learned and healed from so much by being your mother. To little Socrate Aurelius Exantus (aka Bear), my little surprise in life, you are my unpredictable delight in this world.

Most importantly, we would like to thank God for being our rock and refuge. Without God, none of this would be possible, because we are not the main characters.

TESTIMONIALS

Socrate has been a close friend since 1999. Over the last 15 years, he has influenced a change in my life, and I've witnessed his impact on the lives of many others that I know. His influence and support encouraged my wife and me to open our own business. Socrate has continually encouraged and guided us through the last few years, and we now have a successful business. Starting our own business has truly changed our lives for the better, and without Socrate's support and inspiration, I may have never left corporate America to pursue my dreams of owning a successful business.

Socrate has a drive and enthusiasm for leadership, advancement, and success, and if you spend any time with him, you will recognize it immediately. I've watched him build amazing teams in his own businesses, and I've observed how he invests in his employees and their success; it is evident that his employees are loyal and truly love him. He not only invests in his team, but he also gives back to his community and encourages others to do the same. Socrate is a true leader who goes above and beyond by encouraging and educating those that look to him, and he builds them up to be leaders as well. He continually educates himself with the teachings of some of the brightest leaders of our time, and he applies these teachings to life and business. Seeing how Socrate cares for others and invests in their success, it is easy to understand why he is such a success. If you have the opportunity to spend some time with Socrate, you will see that you've made an investment in your own success.

Darryl Gichia-Broussard
CEO, All County Preferred

Over the years, I've had the pleasure to work closely with both Socrate and Cassandra. Time and time again, they have continued to outperform every benchmark and propel their businesses to new heights. I am in awe of their dedication, not only to their organization, but also especially toward each other and their family. I have worked closely with many family-run businesses over the years, and I can say that finding a balance between work and family is not an easy task. They not only have found a way to make it work, but they have excelled in every category. They are big thinkers and share a vision that is fueled by their passion for doing the right thing and helping others to succeed. Socrate and Cassandra have the unique ability to step into an organization and motivate, encourage, and lead people toward achieving their dreams, both personally and professionally. I highly endorse them for any organization.

Todd Bryant
Partner, Signature Wealth Advisors

Socrate Exantus is one of the best communicators that I know. I'm not kidding when I say he's up there with the best in the business. And he practices what he teaches, evidenced by the several successful businesses that he owns and leads. The reason for his success is the clarity and passion that he has for his vision and values, his strategic planning, his genuine care, and his inspiring leadership.

He is a very humble person who sees the best in others and always tries to learn from them. And in the midst of his tremendous business accomplishments, he is a dedicated husband and father. I am confident that working with Socrate will help you to go to the next level in your personal and business life.

Robin Lewis
Executive Director, John Maxwell Team
CEO, Robin Lewis Insurance Organization

Table of Contents

ACKNOWLEDGMENTS 3
    From Cassandra: *4*
TESTIMONIALS 7
Introduction – The Hedgehog Concept 13
My WHy 17

SECTION 1:

The Foundation 21

Chapter 1:
Faith It to Make It 23
    Learning as You Lead *24*
    Does Faith Have to Make Sense? *26*

Chapter 2:
Take Initiative 29
    Procrastination *33*

Chapter 3:
Goals 37
    Measuring Success *41*
    1. Online Reviews *43*
    2. Surveys *46*
    3. Measuring Profitability *48*

Chapter 4:
Prioritize 53
    Creating a System 55
    Master Your Tasks 59
    Delegation 59
        How to Delegate Tasks Effectively: 60

Chapter 5:
Win/Win 65
    Not Always a Win-Win 67
    Committed to Your Values 69

Chapter 6:
Active Listening 77
    Consultative Approach 78
    Recognizing the Value of Your Team 81
    Copreneurs 83
        V-A-L-U-E 84

Chapter 7:
Synergy 87
    When There Is No Synergy 89
    Building Our Team 91
    Creating Synergy 94
    Synergy as Copreneurs 96

Chapter 8:
Grow 99
    Leadership Training 100
    Growth=Life 103

SECTION 2:

The Pillars 107

Chapter 9:
Integrity 109
    Integrity in Action 110
    When Integrity Doesn't Make Sense 113

Chapter 10:
Accountability 119
    What Are Your Vital Signs? 120
    Accountability Measures 123

Chapter 11:
Communication 129
    Communicating as a Value 130
    Team Building 136

Chapter 12:
Teamwork 139
    Principle-Based Decision Making 139
    Understanding the Stages of Team Development 142
    Maximizing Teamwork 146

SECTION 3:

The Capstone 149

Chapter 13:
Sacrifice 151
    Sacrifices That Lead to Success 154

Chapter 14:
Legacy 159
    Leaving Your Mark 160
    Our Children 165

Conclusion 169

About the Authors 173

Introduction – The Hedgehog Concept

Brad Stevens, current head coach of the Boston Celtics, was introduced to the game of basketball at an early age—receiving a basketball hoop for his eighth birthday. His father would often drive him to Bloomington, Indiana, to watch the Indiana Hoosiers basketball games. Stevens played basketball throughout his youth and was his high school's star player, setting school records for career scoring, assists, steals, and three-point field goals. After high school, he ended up at DePauw University on an academic scholarship where he met his wife, who is now his agent. After attending DePauw University, he was recruited by Eli Lilly and became a marketing executive. The multibillion-dollar pharmaceutical company viewed him as a rising star. He was making an excellent salary for a 23-year-old, but he knew that it was not his calling. While he liked the job at Eli Lilly and was good at it, it was not his passion. He considered this deeply because he knew something that many of us in business have learned, and that is the Hedgehog Concept. (Jim Collins wrote about this concept in a book entitled *Good to Great*.) Have you ever heard of the idea that if you like what you do you will never have to work a day in your life? Allow me to explain further. Imagine a Venn diagram with three circles meeting at one middle point. Essentially, the Hedgehog Concept is the intersection between the following three ideas:

1. What are you deeply passionate about?

2. What can you be the best at (good or great)?

3. What drives your economic engine ($)?

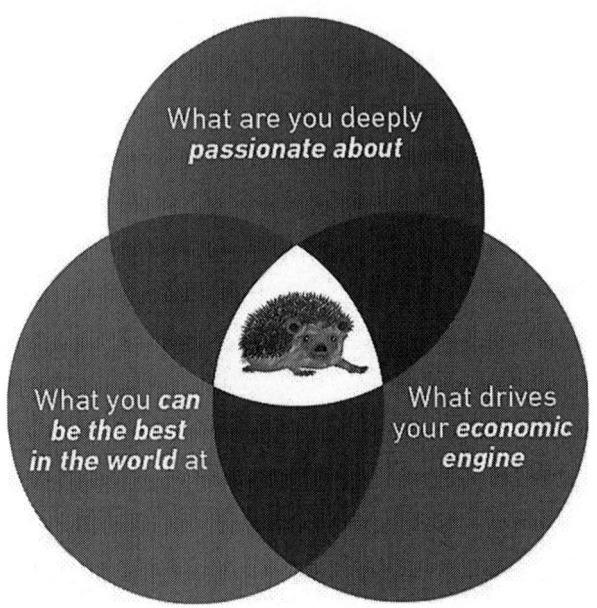

Stevens used his knowledge of this concept and took a leap of faith to accept an unpaid assistant position at Butler University in Indianapolis, Indiana. He planned to wait tables at Applebee's since the original offer was unpaid. But, before he could start at Applebee's, another assistant coach was terminated, and he was offered the position of director of basketball operations for $18,000 per year, a 60 percent pay cut from his salary at Eli Lilly. He was later promoted to full-time assistant coach under Head Coach Todd Lickliter for six years. In 2007, Stevens was named as head coach at Butler University when Lickliter took a job at a more prestigious university.

At age 30, Stevens became the second-youngest coach in Division I. His yearly salary was around $335,000. In his first year, he led Butler to 30 wins, becoming the third youngest head coach in NCAA Division I history to have a 30-win season. He later re-signed for $1.2 million in 2011. At 33 years of age, Stevens became the second-youngest head coach to make an NCAA National Championship game. Moreover, he became the youngest coach to go to two Final Fours. Two!

After leading the university to the best stretch as a coach, Stevens signed a six-year, $22 million contract with the Boston Celtics in 2013. In his second season, he had taken a recently mediocre team to the NBA playoffs—a feat that had not been accomplished by that team in years. Under his leadership, Boston continued to climb, finishing the 2016 season with the best record in the Eastern Conference, only losing to the Cleveland Cavaliers in the Eastern Conference finals. Stevens has reloaded his roster, and the team had one of the best records in the NBA in 2018. They are poised to go deep into the playoffs with a chance to go to the national finals in 2019.

During many interviews with Stevens, you'll often hear him give credit to the numerous mentors and teachers he has had. Most importantly, he credits his success to his faith, family, and following his *hedgehog*. It turns out that passion alone is not enough.

Likewise, for every person and every business to achieve and maintain success, they need to **find their hedgehog**. Here's how:

4. If you are passionate about a job/career and you can be great at it, but you cannot make any money to survive, we call that a **hobby**. Many people believe their hobbies can be a career or a successful business. There is nothing wrong with having a hobby, just don't confuse it with a business or a career.

5. If you are passionate about your job/career, and you can make lots of money doing it, but you are not great or even good at it, this is what we call a **dream**. Unfortunately, it may not last, and, eventually, you may get fired.

6. Lastly, if you have a career/job that you can make a great living doing, and you are great at it, but you are not passionate about, you will not like waking up every morning to go to the office. That is called a **job**. If you are lucky, you may have the courage to leave before you get stuck like Brad Stevens did. You see, the more money you make in corporate America or in a business, the harder it is to leave and start over.

In business as in life, you must find your hedgehog so that as you live out your passion, you will never feel like you are working. Likewise, just as finding your hedgehog is vital to business success, so is finding your reason why: **Why do you do what you do?**

My WHy

It was May 2004, just one month after marrying my best friend and my longtime love, when I decided to alter the course of my life yet again, but this time it was not my personal life but my professional one. I took what was the biggest career risk of my life at the time, voluntarily taking a 50 percent cut in salary and joining a new business unit within the Sprint Corporation to expand my knowledge of business and continue to grow. Now, you must be wondering if I was either crazy or knew ahead of time that I would have a successful outcome. Neither of these scenarios applied. You see, I had been in the same business unit for eight years. I started as an entry-level account representative and moved up to become a Team Leader. Then, an opportunity arose where I was asked to join the Human Resource Training Department, which required that I travel across the country to train new hires and existing employees on Sprint's culture, system, products, and services. I excelled in this role and later earned the position of Training Manager and Leadership Consultant. My next stop was as Marketing Manager, managing multimillion-dollar marketing projects. However, something was missing for me; there was a part of me that wanted something more.

So, with my wife's support, I took the leap of faith, as they say. The reality is—I took a huge pay cut to join Sprint's business unit as an Account Executive. I did not know precisely how I was going to climb back up the ladder, but I knew someone who did. So, I solicited the help of a couple of mentors who were well-versed in business and leadership. Quite frankly, I sought them out because I saw in them a lifestyle example that I wanted to follow. One of them was Monty Pollard, the senior vice president of Sprint. Monty was my business idol. He reported directly to the president of the company. Monty managed over 10,000 people and had been an executive for over 15 years. Surprisingly, he agreed to be my mentor. So, for the next four years, we met every month. Within that time, my salary nearly tripled. I went from being an Account Manager to a Sales Manager to a Regional Sales Manager to a Senior Operations Manager for that business department. However, the most remarkable thing about this mentor relationship was not my progression in the company, but how I found my why.

I had many calls with Monty, but on one particular call, he said something that altered the trajectory of my career. The call started with me asking a simple question: "What was your biggest regret?" He paused. Since we were talking over the phone, I could not see his face, but I could hear the emotion in his voice when he began speaking. He told me the story of a time when he and his wife were driving down a road, not too far from home, and he pointed out a high school to her. His wife turned to him and said, "That is where your son played in the district basketball game." He went on to tell me that while he believed in me and knew that I could achieve whatever I set my mind to, he advised me never to let what's most important be at the mercy of my least important priorities.

The funny thing is that my wife and I did not have any children at that time. However, I knew that my why had changed. Monty's story resonated with me because my parents were not able to attend most of my school activities during my school days. They were hardworking foreigners who had to work two, sometimes three, jobs just to make ends meet. I don't fault them, but I knew that I wanted something different for my life and my future children. So, for the next three to four years, Cassandra and I worked on our exit strategy from corporate America, which was not easy. I learned that the more money you make and the higher your position in corporate America, the harder it is to leave.

In early 2009, I began seriously thinking about leaving the company that I had been with for 14 years—the company that groomed me to become a Senior Manager. Unfortunately, my high-ranking position in the company meant that it was doubtful I would be asked to leave, which meant that I would have to volunteer to go if I wanted to make a change in my career. There were two choices I had before me. If I planned my exit well, I could walk away with a severance package, which would include nearly one year of pay, allowing me to follow my passion and work for myself, but if my plan did not pan out, I would walk away with nothing more than my 401(k)/stock options. Although I had been saving for over eight years, I knew that I could not start a business and support a family of four with our lifestyle for too long with just my savings alone. So, I waited for the right opportunity to present itself. The moment I heard that voluntary separation packages were being offered, I took a very critical action that would set in motion the events that would reveal my new destiny and ultimately lay the path for my legacy.

When the day finally arrived for me to give my resignation notice, I battled fear, anxiety, and doubt. I thought about my wife Cassandra and our children; I didn't want to let them down. What motivated me was the knowledge that Cassandra believed in me. "Even if we lost everything and had to move into a two-bedroom apartment, as long as we are together, we will be fine," she told me that morning. This was a confirmation of the vows that we made to each other just five years prior: For better or for worse, for richer or poorer, she would stand with me.

I entered my office as a man on a mission—a mission to begin the next chapter of my career—to find my hedgehog. With my resignation in hand, I faced the unknown world of business ownership...

SECTION 1:

The Foundation

Chapter 1:

Faith It to Make It

Thoughts of faith are often immediately accompanied by thoughts of religion or a church setting with a priest or pastor standing atop a platform reading from the Bible. Yet, my thoughts of faith go far beyond these images. I am keenly aware of the single story regarding faith. My definition stretches beyond that. Faith is the belief in the unseen, belief not based on proof. It is the complete trust or confidence in someone or something. At first glance, faith may not make sense at all.

Whether you're a believer in God or not, most people have some kind of faith. The universal action taken by everyone who has some level of faith is that many of us will draw upon that faith in times of struggle or times of life-changing decisions.

My family's story is one of faith. My parents are from Haiti, and I was born there, but I grew up in South Florida. It took a significant amount of faith on the part of my parents to uproot our family from their homeland and immigrate to a foreign land. Even though my parents had never been to the United States, they had the faith that there would be more opportunities here.

Everyone exercises some level of faith—whether it is faith in God, faith to start a business, faith to move to a new country, or faith in a job position. Your faith will catapult you to successes you couldn't achieve or experience without it.

Learning as You Lead

In the late '90s, when I was only 21 years old, I was promoted to a leadership role for the Training Department for Sprint, a Fortune 100 company at that time. I have always been a pretty confident young man, and I was very confident in this new position. Yet, the concept of leadership for me was still new. Fortunately, I had excellent leaders around me who noticed my willingness to grow. I learned from some good leaders, and I also learned from some not-so-good leaders. All the advice—both good and bad—served me well at the time. (Until I became a more experienced leader, I didn't realize some of it had been bad advice.) Over the 17-plus years and different leadership positions, I learned a lot from a series of events, experiences, training, and education.

"When a student is ready, the teacher will appear."

As a young professional, I vividly remember an event that changed my professional confidence—an experience where I had to access that faith I previously spoke about, and trust in it. I met with a director by the name of Andy Johnson, and I asked him, "I don't have the experience to lead this team, what do I do?" He replied, "Fake it to make it!" He went on to say that if I simply pretended I knew what I was talking about and acted like it, eventually, I would figure it out. For years I applied this phrase he taught me to every area in business, and it served me well. I went on to continue learning and gaining experiences and increasing my overall competency as a leader.

My leadership competencies flourished when I was "faking it to make it," and I felt confident. However, my confidence waned when I was placed in an environment where I lacked knowledge. In short, I felt uncomfortable and out of my comfort zone. So, this theory did not always work for me. Furthermore, not knowing what the outcome would be when I did "fake it" left me uneasy about how far I actually could go faking it. It was like playing Russian roulette with my confidence. I needed something more. This "more" came in the form of faith: the belief that I was meant to be where I was at the time; the belief that I have more in me than I even know, more than my preparations, more than what other people told me I could do. My faith had to be in my God-given talent to be successful in business—and not my own strength. Period.

Fifteen years later after leaving the business I was working in, I started my own business in the property management field. I had just opened my office and had been in business for about seven months. I wanted to pass on the knowledge I had received in business and leadership to another up-and-coming young man like myself, so I began attempting to coach a young man who was also one of the employees in my company. Consequently, it turned out that while I was expecting to teach him many lessons, he unexpectedly taught me something that I had never learned before. I shared my vision and strategy with this young man, and I told him that there was no guarantee that my approach would work, saying we must fake it to make it. He responded and said, "I have known you for over 10 years, and you're not faking anything. You're leading by faith." Then he said, "You 'faith' it to make it." Suddenly, an enthusiasm leapt inside me. I'm sure the phrase had been said before, but I had never heard it, and it intrigued me.

This young man is now the Vice President of Sales for my Orlando office, the top performing office in the country. There's a big difference between "faking" something and "faithing" something. Faith is based on a belief, but when you fake something, it is not based on a belief.

Does Faith Have to Make Sense?

Faith is the complete trust or confidence in someone or something without proof. Faith sometimes makes no sense at all. From a business perspective, sometimes people have faith, and you wonder where it came from because they may not appear to have all the right tools to succeed in business.

Indeed, what we call faith may look different in everyone's life. However, we all come to a realization that faith is sometimes necessary because we're not going to have all of the projections for starting a business; we're not going to have all the knowledge or all the resources. That's why it takes faith.

Now fast-forward to 2012 when my wife and I decided to open our second office in South Florida. We had seen some success with the first office; naturally, we wanted to leverage that success with a second office. We decided to launch in the South Florida market because both Cassandra and I went to high school in South Florida. It was one of the hardest hit areas during the market crash in 2007, which meant that investors were still descending on South Florida to purchase properties with a high return. Therefore, it was still a buyer's market. Strategically, this move to open a new office made sense to both Cassandra and me. And it made sense to us because of our faith in God—our faith to make our business successful not only for our family but for others as well.

After we launched the second office, I can remember having a conversation with a woman that changed my thinking about the main reason we had achieved some success. It was really about faith, but I had forgotten that my success came from my faith. I sat across a table from Sylvia Madison, an insurance agent who was likely in her 50s or so. She was incredibly passionate about her field of work and had what I would call a customer service-oriented personality. Sylvia insisted on meeting me in person to discuss my insurance needs, although we could have addressed them over the phone. Before we began discussing what policies I needed for my business, which would include errors and omissions, general liability, workers' comp, etc., she said, "Socrate, you're doing well for opening your second office in just three years. To what do you attribute your success?" I had not really given much thought to what we attributed our growth because I didn't consider what we were doing as a success. Our business growth mindset was such that we were not already a success, but it was something we were constantly working toward.

I humbly replied to her, "We are part of great franchise system, and we have a great team. We have a great strategy, and I think that God played a role in our success." She stopped me and said, "No, he did not." Of course, I was stunned by her response because I consider myself a believer. I thought that I would surely be struck by lightning or something if I did not acknowledge God's role in what we were doing.

Sylvia further explained, "God did not play a role. He is the main character, and you and your team are playing a role." I paused for a few seconds to let what she said to me sink in because it didn't really register the first time. Then, I realized that she was right. In fact, she was more than right. I had not recruited many of the people that decided to join me in my business. Instead, many of them found me. The same thing occurred with many of the clients that we landed; they came to us. So, we cannot take full credit for any of it. At best, I can say that my team and I were positioned well to play our parts. We are all playing out specific roles in our lives.

This conversation with my insurance agent also removed a huge burden off my shoulders to relinquish control. It was because of faith that I realized that I simply needed to do my best and play my role.

So, did my faith catapult my business growth? The answer to that question is an unequivocal…yes!

Chapter 2:

Take Initiative

> "It is not often that a man can make opportunities for himself. But he can put himself in such shape that when or if the opportunities come he is ready."
>
> ~Theodore Roosevelt

The well-known idiom "take initiative" has been used multiple times over the years to describe the act of stepping out boldly and proactively to take action. Taking initiative is an attribute that can directly affect your level of success in all areas of life, especially business, either positively or negatively. So, the question to ask would then be: What is the first step in applying this idiom to your business?

Let me begin by first telling you a story. I decided at one point in my business career that I really wanted to find a mentor. I did, and her name was Beverly Pindling. She taught the ethics course at the local realtor board in Orlando. And she was incredible—she gave me little nuggets of wisdom that would later impact my life and what it meant to take initiative. During our first lunch meeting, she asked me a question. "Cassandra, in order to make it in this business, you have got to learn to set yourself apart. How are you going to present yourself? How are you going to make yourself unique in this industry?" I immediately began considering my answers to her questions. I wanted to impress her by trying to come up with a really great answer. I said, "I'm going to go out there and do the best that I can. I'll be the best that I can be and provide my clients with the best customer service in the world." She chuckled, looked at me, and said, "You know what, that's all good and dandy Cassandra, but that's not the right answer." I was kind of deflated, to be quite honest, because I really wanted to impress her. She then asked me, "What if your best is not good enough?"

> **It's not always about having all the answers. It's about being proactive and not reactive.**

When she asked me that question, it gave me great pause. She told me that I had to do all I could do to be the best. She advised that I should consistently assess my efforts and ask myself if I am already doing all that I can do to be the best. I quickly realized that those types of questions were questions that every business owner, including myself, should always ask of themselves. Because what if your best isn't good enough?

Often, we hear people say that they do the best they can do. However, if we were to go back and assess certain situations, we

realize that many things could have been done to help prevent a negative outcome. What if every business owner took this approach to every obstacle and every business problem? Dan Oswald, writer for *The Oswald Letter*, addressed the topic of insights and business leadership when he said that it was more important to ask the right questions than it was to always have the answer. His reasoning behind this insightful nugget of wisdom was that it is the questions that allow people to assess a situation. "None of us can have all the answers, especially if we haven't asked any questions. Questions shed light on a situation. Questions add context to a situation. Questions provide data that help draw the correct conclusion," he said.

Usually, when a business is addressing an issue, it's too late if they are dealing with the symptoms of the issue rather than dealing with the original issue itself. The key is to be proactive when assessing situations. In my line of work in property management, we are always in situations where we are talking to people and dealing with an issue. The trouble is that we often deal with the issue after the fact, meaning what may have begun as a small problem then turns into a big problem and eventually into a big mess to clean up. Yet, there were many opportunities when we first learned of the issue, and it could have been addressed and remedied then, which is why I have such a passion for being proactive.

When you think that you've done your best, you should still sit back and continue to assess your steps and what you did or did not do correctly. Inevitably, you will find that there will be times when you really didn't do all that you could. This was where I found myself when I was faced with an ongoing issue that kept coming up in our business.

Our team would meet on a weekly basis to discuss the health of our business. I would dread the meetings because it was like pulling teeth to get answers about not achieving our goals or missed opportunities. No one knew what was really happening in his or her portfolio. The team did not have a clear understanding of how to measure success. I remembered Beverly saying, "Have you done all that you can do?" I had to ask myself a few questions.

- How do we measure success?
- What important activities are required to achieve our goals?
- How do we track the results?
- How do we hold the team accountable?

I realized it was my fault; I never communicated how they were being measured or what they were being graded on. Weekly meetings became frustrating because we were always rallying the team to come up with a plan to put out fires. The next meeting would be about a new issue. I was in a constant reactive mode. Many leaders can relate to the anxiety that comes with not knowing what is coming next. Something had to change. Identifying the problem doesn't always mean you have to come up with all the answers. It means you ask the right questions and go digging for the right answers. You don't have to do it on your own either. If you have ever watched a WWF wrestling match, it means you can tag a partner in to help you. My partner was Socrate. He listened to me list our team's issues and the areas we were constantly struggling in. Socrate created ***vital signs*** as the solution. Vital signs are an accountability tool that allowed us to clearly define our goals and expectations. We were able to track results, and our team clearly understood how we measured success. Now the next step was getting everyone to use the tool and ensure the reports were accurate. (Socrate discusses vital signs in detail in Chapter 10 — Accountability.)

Procrastination

What is most important should never come at the mercy of what's least important. Avoiding the things that we don't like to do and leaving them to the last minute will inevitably backfire. When procrastination rears its ugly head, you end up being in reactive mode trying to clean up the mess that exudes. And that's exactly what happened to me in the situation I discussed previously with my team. And the plot thickens. So how can you overcome procrastination?

The best analogy I can think of is that of watching a movie—a movie you've seen before. You know all the characters and the story line and can describe every scene in detail. You ultimately know how the movie will end. Being reactive or procrastinating is like watching a movie filled with suspense for the first time. You are anxious and sitting on the edge of your seat in anticipation. Why? Because you have no idea what is going to happen next. You react to every scene as it unfolds.

Let me set up the scene for you. We identified a problem in our business earlier, and we came up with a tool to address it, right? Ta, da – vital signs! We implemented the tool with the team and decided that each property manager would do a monthly presentation on it. Several parts of the report relied on data from multiple departments, and everyone was assigned a role in completing the report. The first few months, the reports were incomplete or inaccurate, and I was getting frustrated again. (Does this movie seem eerily familiar?) Key individuals would not do their part or check to see if it had been completed correctly. Socrate would ask me why this was not getting done. I went into my dialogue of what everyone was not doing and how people were dropping the ball, and he would stop me and say, "You are to blame." I was shocked. Me? I was doing everything I was supposed to do. I was the idea woman. I had a lot of great ideas, but when it came to execution, I had a lot of excuses.

> **What's most important should never be at the mercy of what's least important.**

Socrate likened the situation to a group assignment in school. If you wanted an A, you needed to make sure everyone did his or her part because if one person didn't, then the assignment was incomplete. Worse yet, if you had a hard-nosed professor, he just may not accept the assignment at all, and you would get an F. I had procrastinated and waited until the last minute to receive the information from everyone.

The truth is sometimes we procrastinate to avoid confrontation. We don't want to come across like a nag. We fall into the trap of wanting everyone to like us. We don't want to hold people accountable. Can anyone relate to this character?

In Patrick Lencioni's book, *The Five Dysfunctions of a Team*, he illustrates this beautifully. His fictional character Kathryn has the painful task of showing a team that was disjointed and ineffective how to reset and become a team that produces. She has several offsite meetings to uncover how each of them contributed to the current state of their dysfunction. Everyone points fingers at each other.

As leaders, we always want to take credit when our team does well. Conversely, we often shift blame to the players on our team when they fall short. The book talks about the absence of ac-

countability and the fear of conflict as a part of the dysfunction. Is this a scene that you have seen play out in your business or your organization? The absence of accountability creates an environment where no one calls each other out for not doing what everyone agreed to do. The fear of conflict is when we want to avoid that interpersonal conflict at all costs, even to say to a team member or peer, "That does not meet our standard" or, "We have to do better." Sometimes that person is you. Are you willing to hear that message to get to the next level?

Well, my fellow movie watchers, let's recap what we know about this movie.

1. Let's review the movie again. (Assess the situation.)

2. Who are my characters? (Identify the key players.)

3. What is the plot? (Create a timeline.)

4. Rewrite the end of the movie. (What's needed to change the narrative?)

To assess the situation, again I use Beverly's words: "Have I done all that I can do?" You want to first evaluate the situation by asking questions relative to it. Questions like: What is the issue? How can the issue be solved? Instead, I was procrastinating. I waited until the last minute and never took the time to review the work to ensure that it was correct.

I had to set a deadline by which tasks were to be completed and give ample time to review the report myself to ensure accuracy. I had to inspect what I expected.

Now, I can tell you this; I know how the movie ends. The student (me) gets an A on the assignment because it is turned in on time and complete. And everyone is doing his or her part.

> **In order to lead a team you have to check your ego at the door.**

You also have to accept responsibility when you or your team does not perform. Take the initiative and don't procrastinate. Leave your, "I want to be liked," card at home. Fear of confrontation will win you likes, but you will lose each other's respect. Don't be afraid to raise the bar and call your team out when they don't meet expectations. Being reactive creates an unpredictable way of being. It breeds anxiety and frustration, two emotions that do not look good on a leader. You may have worked with or know someone like this. Maybe that person could be you. How do you change it? Ask yourself if you have you done all that you can do. BE proactive, NOT reactive.

Chapter 3:

Goals

> "What you get by achieving your goals is not as important as what you become by achieving your goals."
>
> ~Henry David Thoreau

Goal setting is important—not only for personal endeavors but even more so for business endeavors. Every entrepreneur you meet will most likely describe to you how critical goal setting is to your continued success. But what is the objective of setting a goal? Is it to show the world that you can do what you said you would do—to be the best at anything—or is it to change you for the better? Hmm, it's definitely something to consider. Prominent leader, entrepreneur, and speaker John Maxwell has given lots of advice on success and goal setting, and his most poignant advice on goal setting is this:

> *"Don't ever be impressed with goal setting; be impressed with goal getting. Reaching new goals and moving to a higher level of performance always requires change, and change feels awkward. But take comfort in the knowledge that if a change doesn't feel uncomfortable, then it's probably not really a change."*

Reading a quote like this certainly causes you to wonder if the objective is actually goal setting and not simply setting a vision for what success will look like for you and putting things in place to see that vision come to pass.

In 2007, my coworker Rufus' mother passed away. Her name was Mrs. Mosley, and I had met her a few times at his home, but I had limited conversations with her during those few encounters. Rufus was more than a coworker; he was a friend. I wanted to show my respect and attend his mother's funeral to support him. Mrs. Mosley was a retired educator in Eustis, Florida, a small town just northwest of Orlando. She began her career as a teacher and later became a school administrator. She ended her career as the assistant principal at Eustis High School. Surprisingly, at 32 years old, I had never been to a funeral before. I guess I've been lucky because I have not experienced the death of many loved ones. That Saturday morning, I had to take that 45-minute drive to the funeral alone because Cassandra couldn't make it. I was so surprised to see that over 1,000 people attended Mrs. Mosley's funeral. I thought it would be a small gathering of family and friends, but that was far from the life celebration that I witnessed through all those who attended.

When I arrived at the church, I greeted Rufus and his wife and then slowly walked away from them to my seat, not knowing the right words to speak to them after such a devastating loss. As I sat at the back of the church, I watched and listened.

I heard dozens of prominent people speak about Mrs. Mosley. Each person had their own story of the impact that she had on their lives. The speakers were fellow educators, friends, or colleagues. A number of the speakers were her former students who were now businessmen and women, doctors, attorneys, and Eustis city officials.

The common theme among them was this: She added value to their lives. Many said that, but for Mrs. Mosley, they would not be where they were in life. She never told people what they wanted to hear, but she often told them what they needed to hear. She was tough.

The celebration and speeches went on for two hours. Although this was supposed to be the end of life for Mrs. Mosley, I quickly realized that Mrs. Mosley's legacy would live on in the lives of those she impacted, who are now affecting even more lives.

I then understood what Stephen Covey meant when he said, "Begin with the end in mind." I always thought of that statement as one that only referred to how you wanted your business to end, but Mrs. Mosley's funeral crystallized the real meaning of that quote to me, which was to begin or live your life always thinking about how it will end. How will you be changed and how will your life impact others for a positive change?

At the end of Mrs. Mosley's celebration, I rushed to my car to call Cassandra to tell her how amazing it had been. She said, "What do you mean? I thought you went to a funeral?" I replied, "I did, but it was not what I expected. I went to a life celebration of a remarkable person who clearly began her life with the end in mind."

I went on to tell her that if I have a quarter of that many people at my funeral who speak as passionately about me as they did about her and the difference she made in their lives, then I would consider myself a success.

From that day forward, my goals changed from simply becoming a successful person to asking myself how I could add value to people and have a positive impact on their lives to leave a legacy.

Fast-forward three years later to 2010, a month after I left corporate America. Cassandra and I had decided to become business owners and purchase the east Orlando territory for this little franchise called All County Property Management. There were only seven franchises before we signed. As we were interviewing the corporate office to decide if we wanted to buy into their system, they were also interviewing us to determine whether we were the right fit. I can remember driving to Tampa to meet with the founders, Sandy and Scott. During the one-day meeting, they asked me what my goal was as a franchisee. Having been in leadership for years and coming from the corporate world, I knew that I wanted something perhaps different than what other franchisees who came before me wanted. I said, "My goal is to be benchmark franchisee for All County and to be the standard for the All County system."

By the look on their faces, I knew that my response was both different and refreshing because they wanted bold and driven people in the system. I learned as a leader that if your goal is to focus on adding value to people, you will achieve success and get a group of people to buy into that philosophy. You can achieve almost any business goal and objective. The key is to remove the focus on you as a leader and instead focus on your team.

Measuring Success

When I studied business at the University of Central Florida, I learned that there are really four business functions from a managerial perspective: **planning, organizing, leading, and control**. If you focus on the team, then it's easier to manage these four major business functions. Planning is about setting a goal and having expectations. Organizing is putting it all together and prioritizing. Leading is how you affect and impact change in people and gain buy-ins. Control is how you measure success, along with the tools, resources, and accountability you use to manage that control. It's important to involve whomever you have on your core team to help set the goals and define the actions necessary to achieve those goals. (At times, this may be difficult to involve others, but at least solicit feedback once you, as a leader, define the goals and objectives.)

In the beginning, my core team was only Cassandra and me. Over the years, however, my core team has increased in size, but the process remains the same when setting goals. One of the most important ways to set goals is to ask yourself how you will measure success. In other words, what is your end goal? I've met a lot of business owners, and many of them can't answer that question.

When it comes to setting goals, I've learned that the first critical step is to set a vision. Next, you must break down your goals or objectives to quantifiable and qualifiable objectives. I took two courses in my undergrad studies that helped me understand the importance of creating smart goals: One was on quantitative tools, and one was on qualitative tools.

Quantitative tools help you ensure that there's a way to measure the key performance indicators. Qualitative tools help you identify the things that are not easily measurable and find ways to assign numerical values to goals so that you can measure them.

Goals

Following is a list of objectives that Cassandra and I set for our business to gauge whether we were successful.

WE WILL KNOW WE ARE
SUCCESSFUL
WHEN

- Our Owners are RAVING Fans!
- Our Tenants are compliant/rent-payint tenants.
- Our Employees are happy coming into work and are financially rewarded equitably.
- Our vendors truly are partners in our success.
- Our costs remains low and our profit margins are HIGH.
- Our processes are simplified and are followed by our Property Managers.
- We are recognized for our professional expertise in the industry, and in the community!

The chart above is a visual representation of a measurement of success. The objectives listed are high-level goals. Some of them are easily quantifiable goals, and some of them are more qualitative goals that we now have a way to measure. For example, every business, whether retail, information technology, food, or property management must be concerned about four key stakeholders when measuring success:

1. Clients — Are your clients satisfied with your service/product?

2. Employees — Are your employees satisfied?

3. Investors — Are you profitable?

4. Environment — This refers to your contribution to the environment you do business in. Find a way to measure whether you are actually giving back, not just from a philanthropic perspective but by how you're positively impacting your marketplace.

We wanted our business to be centered around the objectives on the success chart. We wanted our owners to be raving fans for a lot of reasons. That was one of our main goals. We also wanted clients that were happy to work with us, not clients who were simply stuck working with us. There's a big difference between a client that is happy to work with you and one that is stuck working with you due to a binding contract.

The difference is this: If your clients are raving fans, they are going to refer your business to others. Believe it or not, a large percentage of our business now comes from our existing clients because we made that one of our top priorities. We did not understand or know how to measure it until about three years ago. The options that could be used to measure it were things like conducting a survey or utilizing the tools of online reputation reviews.

1. Online Reviews

Let's talk a little more about the effectiveness of online reputation reviews for business success ... or even failure. Three years ago, there was a young man that began working with us as one of our Account Managers, and he was about to acquire his first client contract. He was so excited. The owner liked him and liked our company, but the owner had one more criterion. The owner wanted to look online to see how we rated compared to other property management companies in the area. The problem was that we had never focused on online reputation reviews or management before. The only people who were rating us online were tenants who were unhappy with our services. And if someone is unhappy with a company, they will find a way to voice their grievances online through a company review, along with sharing their unsatisfactory experience with family and friends. On the other hand, I learned that in business if someone goes to a restaurant and experiences exceptional service, 95 percent of them are not going to share their positive experience with the manager, fill out a company survey, or share their exceptional experience online in a review.

This was a consideration that Cassandra and I had to take into account for our company. When this new potential owner looked us up online, he found that we didn't have a high online Google review score, which at the time was 2.5 out of a possible 5.0. There were a few positive reviews scattered within the negative ones, but the negative reviews were prevalent. There were some from tenants who were not happy with us, either because they had been evicted or had been charged a fee for paying their rent late. This bothered me because, in the end, this client did not become one of our clients. In fact, this potential new client told my Account Manager outright that he came to the decision not to sign the contract with our company solely based on our negative online rating. This was certainly a big blow to our company and our confidence. For the next six months or so, I could not get this experience out of my mind. So, I decided to take the initiative and be proactive.

I spoke to all my employees about enacting a new campaign: Whenever they delivered exceptional service to a tenant or to a client/owner of an investment property that we managed, they were to ask the client/customer to go online to give us a review of our services. Essentially, we were saying to them, "If you like our services, let us know. If you don't like the services, let us know that too."

Twelve months later, we went from a 2.5 Google review rating with about 10 reviews to having over 255 reviews. Our rating for the Orlando office (led by Reshard Battle) is now at 4.1 (with 192 reviews). Our South Florida office has a rating of 4.2, and our Jacksonville office (lead by Paula Givler) has a rating of 4.0. These are excellent ratings because our industry is notorious for bad reviews from tenants that are unhappy with a late fee or eviction due to nonpayment. We now know that our owners are raving fans; they are posting positive comments online. In addition, our tenants are compliant, rent-paying tenants. When we came up with that objective, we had not really given a whole lot of thought as to how to make that a quantifiable metric. For our industry, it's simple. We are in the business of collecting rent for the properties we manage for our investors who entrust their investment properties or rental properties to us. That metric is an easy one. We look at the rent that we are to collect, and we compare it to what we didn't collect.

For example, if we were supposed to collect $100,000 in rent but instead collected $95,000, then there's a 5 percent delinquency (or 5 percent of the money we did not collect). The industry standard is around 5 percent. We are proud that on a monthly basis our rent delinquency—that's the measure of whether the tenants are compliant and pay rent—is typically around 2.0 percent for multiple locations. Additionally, our employees are

Goals

happy coming into work and are financially rewarded equitably. This leads me to the next option of measuring success, which is a survey for employee satisfaction.

2. Surveys

I thought long and hard about this one, because I did not want to come up with a generic survey that I submitted on a frequent basis to obtain feedback from my employees. Then I met a young man who introduced me to a tool that he uses to complete employee surveys called Officevibe. It allows us to keep a pulse on the culture of our offices in Central Florida as well as in Jacksonville, providing an excellent gauge to how our employees are feeling in their work environment. The way Officevibe works is that once you load all your employees' names into it, a third party will send a survey to every employee. The employee gets to decide if they want to receive the survey every Monday, every Tuesday, or randomly throughout the week. The questions are the same for every employee, but the day or time they receive the survey is different, based on their choosing.

One of the most important aspects of this survey is that it's anonymous. The business owner does not select the questions, nor do they know the employee who is responding. When things aren't going well, I hear about it on a weekly basis through Officevibe, and I can immediately do something about it. My goal as a business owner is to ensure that my employees are satisfied with me as their employer and that they feel rewarded for their time and hard work.

We use two different forms of surveys: **employee surveys** and **vendor surveys**. We send out a monthly survey to a set of clients and tenants. Based on our internal survey results, we would ask certain recipients to review us online, whether through a Google review, Angie's List, or the Better Business Bureau. Our success measurement involves our vendors as well. As a property management company, we subcontract with a lot of vendors. Vendors are partners in our success. When we give business to a vendor, we make sure that they understand that as a company that is providing business to them, we also encourage them to consider us and refer business to us, because as we grow, they will too. We hire vendors in our local market, such as general contractors, electrical companies, air conditioning companies, plumbers, roofers ... you name it. If you can create a partnership with your vendors, and they're looking out for business for you as well, you can build a reciprocal relationship. That's why it's always important to include your business partners and vendors in how you measure success.

One of the biggest deals we received in the Orlando office was a referral from one of our air conditioning vendors. About five years ago, an air conditioning company was out working on an estimate for a quote for a 64-unit apartment complex before the buyer purchased the property. As he was talking to them, he realized they were about to buy this property, but they had not decided on who was going to manage the property. He quickly contacted my team and me and told us about it, recommending we approach the two decision makers. He told us that they did not own the property yet but said when they do, we would want to be the ones managing this property. Well, after two to three months of back-and-forth negotiations, they chose to go with us. That is an example of how vendors can truly be partners in your business success.

3. Measuring Profitability

One of our initial objectives was to keep our costs low and our profit margins high in order to expand beyond one market. We've been able to take a $150,000 investment from our Orlando office and grow to four new markets, reinvesting our profits to expand and provide growth opportunities for our teams. This is the power of profitability. What started as a two-person office has grown to as many as 30 team members, which is evidence of the benefit of profitability measurement.

We are recognized for our professional expertise in the community, and we give back to the community. We use the qualitative tool of surveys, reviews, and feedback to measure our effectiveness as business owners and our customers' assessment of our work.

We use this same qualitative tool to measure owner satisfaction and tenant satisfaction. If our property managers are delivering, then they're doing an excellent job. So, the feedback that we get back from our tenants, who are our customers, and our clients, who are our property owners, will fall in line.

You may be asking how we quantify that feedback. And it's a valid question. Once a year, whether we are in Orlando, South Florida, or Jacksonville, we host a networking event. It is a celebration sponsored by a nonprofit organization, and through it we quantify how much we're giving back to the community. For example, five years ago, we had a grand opening event in the South Florida office to launch this new location. We raised $8,500 in one night. We got the entire community of our vendors, clients, and colleagues to donate to the Susan B. Anthony Recovery Center. This was a wonderful event, and we were also able to measure our contribution to the great organization, which has addiction recovery programs for women. One year before, we hosted a similar event in Orlando where we were doing a basic networking event. We chose to sponsor Habitat for Humanity. In the months leading up to that event, we were involved in the Habit Build week in Central Florida, where we helped raise over $8,000 for Habitat for Humanity. Those are examples of the ways by which we quantify our involvement in the community.

Now, this method of quantifying is nothing new. We're not taking credit for creating this; we are just using tools that we know work. Oftentimes, when companies are raising funds, they'll have a thermometer of a goal they have in mind for the year. Then you can see the marker move up as people donate more. The entire team can celebrate when they reach the goal. Seven years ago, when I opened the office in Orlando, we understood how powerful this type of measurement was. We set a goal, pursued it, and measured our team achievement toward those goals.

> **The world makes way for the man or woman who knows where he or she is going.**

When you determine your goal as a business, and you know how many salespeople you have in the office, you can assign a small portion of that goal to each individual. Essentially, your business or team goal can be broken down into a goal for each person on your team. This is a strategy I utilize in my office. I had all my employees sign a 3- by 2-foot thermometer graphic that we hung on the office wall. Everyone committed to reaching this goal as a team. You can't walk into our office and not see that thermometer. Every time somebody would acquire a new client, we would mark off on the thermometer how much closer we were to reaching our goal. This strategy significantly motivated my team and myself as we were all able to have a visual description of the goal

Goals

we had set for the business and exactly how it would be measured. It took us nearly 10 months, but we finally reached that 100 mark, which represented 100 new properties to manage.

At the time, this was the fastest-growing All County office. No one else had acquired 100 properties in such a short time. I think in large part the reason this strategy worked was that we had our team buy into it and we set up a visual representation of our goal in the office as a daily reminder. Even before our team bought into it, Cassandra and I had. As a company, we understood our hedgehog, and we would not deviate on that or lose focus on our core competency. We knew that we were good at managing properties and had found a commonality between our passion for real estate and managing properties for others. We knew how to make money doing it, and we remained consistent.

This strategy of broadcasting and measuring your results can be likened to a sports game. How would the players play the game if there were not a scoreboard? One would argue that they would not play the same way they play today if there was not a scoreboard. Our thermometer represented a scoreboard for us as a company so that we would know our business growth status. We were not comparing ourselves to other property management companies, but we used the thermometer as our very own scoreboard to reach our personal goal.

We don't chase other companies; we chase our goal. What made this strategy even more powerful was that after that first accomplishment, our team wanted to know what was next. What was our next target? They were eager to set a new milestone.

As a result, we set a new goal to reach another 100 properties. It did not take us 10 months to reach the next milestone; it only took us six months. A year later, we had acquired 200 properties. We celebrated with a huge celebration at a very prestigious club

in downtown Orlando, which really made the team feel a sense of accomplishment that we were able to achieve our milestone in that way.

Setting Goals

There were a few significant steps that we took to accomplish our success. One of these was that after we set our goal, we also set a deadline; a goal needs to have a deadline. With that deadline, you will *pace* yourself and keep track of your successes along the way until you reach that deadline.

Many people may not be familiar with pacing, but it's critical to measuring business performance. For example, when you look at a scoreboard, you're not just looking at the score; you're looking at the time as well because if you're supposed to reach a particular milestone, but you have no time left, that's tough. Conversely, if you're looking at the scoreboard and you're winning, and you've still got a ton of time left, that gives you the opportunity to blow the goal out of the water. Pacing allowed us to do that. As a team, we look at our score. Then, we look to see how we're pacing, which has a lot to do with timing compared to the results.

Simply, the importance of setting a goal and preparing a strategy is that if you know where you're going, you will find people who are willing to join you, whether they are on your team or they're supporters of that goal. The first step in any business is to set your goal. It is that critical. If you want to end up somewhere, first you have to make a declaration of it.

Think of a basketball court example. When you meet with a few people on the basketball court, you want them to know that you want to win. If they don't get a sense of your desire to win, then most likely they won't want to be a part of your team.

It's critical that you have people around you who are convinced of your goal and support you in its execution. One of the first exercises we do as a business team when we hire a new property manager is to explain to them what our goal is and we help them understand why they need to set a personal goal to link our business goal.

If you can get someone to set a goal, then they're more likely to achieve the goal than someone who doesn't set one. Usually, I've found that the reason people don't set goals is that they don't want to be disappointed. It's also the same reason people do set goals—they want to have a sense of accountability.

Goal setting is about establishing a vision and staying on course to see it to completion. Once the vision is set, it's necessary to start breaking it down into quantifiable goals and involving your team. If you're persistent and do this every quarter, every year, year in and year out, you'll develop a culture where goals are common and, therefore, accountability for achieving those goals will be part of the culture that you'll develop.

HEDGEHOG HINTS:

❶ Consider the importance of goals and where your business would be today if you never set goals.

❷ Take steps to create goals for your business.

Chapter 4:

Prioritize

> "Most of us spend too much time on what is urgent and not enough time on what is important."
>
> ~Stephen R. Covey

Hearing the word "priority" normally evokes a message of putting what is important first, above all else. And this is completely accurate. However, prioritizing is an act that is learned and must consistently be practiced every day through an understanding of what is important in your life.

In our business, we had to learn to prioritize in order to accomplish this. After I'd been in business for five years, we wanted to expand our territory. In fact, Cassandra and I often prayed to

God to expand our territory. We knew that expansion was in our sight. However, we were having a difficult time handling two offices—one in Orlando and the other in South Florida. Both offices were doing well, especially the South Florida office. We wanted to excel not only for ourselves but to provide growth opportunities for our employees. We had our future and their future in mind.

There was a lot going on in our minds about growth and why we wanted to grow. The problem is that we got into a situation where we were probably over our heads in terms of how we were handling the day-to-day operations. While we had the funds readily available and had faithful employees, Cassandra and I didn't feel comfortable because we were not handling our business correctly. We needed some sound advice.

So, we met with an attorney who was also a vendor for our business. He gave us sound advice on how to grow a business. He and his partner were managing a successfully growing business and had been using a system that had proven to work.

Then I asked him what system he was using for his business and learned about a system called *Master Your Now*. It is a system that you can use along with Outlook, which helps you to manage your incoming emails, calendar, and tasks.

Master Your Now is not something that I'm promoting. I don't have any vested interest in the system other than the fact that it has really changed how we prioritize tasks and the influx of emails in our business. We have implemented the system in our business, and many of our team members are using the same system to stay organized and prioritize their day to day.

With the Master Your Now system, we found 20 to 30 percent more time in our day to day without having to work later, wake

up earlier, or put in additional hours because we had a system that we were using on a regular basis. Consider this, most people use their emails as their inbox, so lots of information comes in all at once. The problem with that is they don't have any priorities in terms of what's more important and what's least important. The Master Your Now system was a workable system that we could implement immediately to prioritize information coming in and going out.

When we implemented the system, we found that we became more efficient and effective with what we were doing on a day-to-day basis. As a result, two months later we made the decision to open up a third office in Jacksonville, Florida. Had we not implemented the Master Your Now system to prioritize our day to day and our business as a whole, I don't believe Cassandra and I would have had the confidence to go forward with that third office. We couldn't move forward until we realized or learned how to better prioritize and "master our now."

Creating a System

Now, not every business will choose to use the Master Your Now system. Regardless of what system a business chooses, it is still necessary to master the art of prioritizing in your business. The objective is to figure out what has to be done now and get more hours out of your day by focusing on the more important tasks/projects.

The first step you must take is to determine and utilize a system that identifies everything that comes into your inbox as important, unimportant, urgent, or nonurgent. I think the mistake that a lot of people make is thinking that every message that comes into their inbox should be given the same weight, the same scale in terms of how important it is.

For example, an individual may spend too much time on an email, responding to something that is not as important as payroll. Everything that comes into your inbox does not need to have the same level of importance or urgency. I learned from Stephen Covey that in order to put first things first and to prioritize properly, you must be able to identify the urgency level of tasks or phone calls that hit your desk on a daily basis.

I'll give you the perfect example. One of the first things that I do every morning is check my voicemail. The purpose of checking my voicemail every day is not so that I can return every single phone call right away, because some of the calls that I get may be a salesperson calling me about a product/service that we do not need, but so that I can respond to the most urgent messages. This is an example of prioritizing your time by organizing voicemails.

Let's look at the email program Outlook, for example. Outlook is a tool, which like any other technology can be a savior or it can be a detriment to your success. It's all in how you prioritize it. Many people spend an enormous amount of time in Outlook just looking for the next email that comes in so they can respond to it. What the Master Your Now system helps you do is prioritize the time it takes to look at your email and focus on the tasks that you have on your list of things to do. It enables you to handle the most important things first, then reassigns tasks based on more emails that come in to determine what you do next and so on.

A lot of people leave every email in their inbox, and there's no sense of priority. I would say 50 percent of the emails that I get contain information that I need to know, but I don't need to act on each one immediately. Many times, I'll quickly read them and file them just so that they are not sitting in my inbox. If I have a task that I need to do with that email, I'll skim through that email quickly. If that is a task that I can respond to or accomplish within five minutes, then it will get done. If it requires 30 or more minutes or even 15 minutes of my time, I will have to make it a task that I'm going to do either later in the day or schedule it for a later date/time with a deadline.

Being proactive and productive with messages throughout your day means that you shouldn't have email open all day long. I try to look at email two to four times a day, sometimes a little more depending upon what's going on. I give myself a 30-minute time frame to read my emails, process them, prioritize the most and least important, and then respond to people appropriately. I know my tasks and my priorities, and email is not always a priority. We live in a culture where when somebody sends me an email, they expect an immediate response for some reason. And sometimes, immediate responses just can't happen.

Here's an example of how I prioritize a typical morning. My first task in the morning is checking voicemails, which are usually the most important things that will come through your business, so after I listen to them, I prioritize them. I respond to some of them right away. Like I said earlier, if it's a quick phone call, perhaps five minutes, I'll make that call, but if it's a longer conversation that I need to have with someone, I may add that to my Outlook tasks on the computer. The second thing that I'll do is quickly skim through my emails and get rid of the things that are junk while filing the things that I know are important but don't need my immediate action. Following that, I'll begin to take a more thorough look at my emails and decide if it's a task that I need to schedule for that day or if it's a task that can be scheduled to be done at a later date. By doing that, I can quickly clean my inbox and only work from my task list.

Prioritize

Cassandra and I have a little fun managing our email. Once a week, I'll check with her and say, "How many emails do you have in your inbox today?" Sometimes it's important to have a reminder or an accountability partner that will have some fun with your emails and say, "How are you managing your now, or how many emails do you have in your inbox?" We get excited when we end the day, and there are very few emails in our inbox.

The point in creating a system of prioritizing essential and nonessential messages for your business is getting your email messages down to zero. This statement alone is a reason for shock and awe in the business world and is mostly considered impossible. I'm sure even you are saying to yourself right now, "Do you know how many emails I get every day?" The reality is it can be done; you *can* get your email messages down to zero. But this will only happen if you've got a system. The system only works if you know your priorities.

If we had not created a system of prioritizing our messages for our business, then we probably wouldn't have moved forward with our third office. Currently, our third office is exceeding all expectations. Also, focusing on prioritizing is what will allow you to do more and grow your business, and then do even more.

I learned a long time ago working with successful senior executives who were two or three levels above me that they had systems for prioritizing important things. The Master Your Now system was not around during that time, but they proved to me that systems of prioritizing really work and allow people like you and me to be able to get a lot more done in an eight- or nine-hour day. In a 24-hour schedule, a system like this allows us to get a lot more done than the average person. As a result, we can do so much more and accomplish so much more.

Master Your Tasks

Every success begins with how you prioritize the things that are coming at you on a daily basis to the extent that you can master them instead of them mastering you. Two and a half years ago, I didn't think I could or wanted to open a third office because I didn't know how I was going to be able to handle the influx of emails, phone calls, and issues that I needed to deal with daily. However, having a system to prioritize absolutely made that possible.

In John Maxwell's book, *Developing a Leader Within You*, he addressed the Pareto principle, which is the 80/20 Rule. This rule states that 80 percent of your results come from 20 percent of your activities. John Maxwell was the first person I encountered who put it in a graphical form for me to clearly understand. Therefore, if you would spend 80 percent of your time on the top 20 percent of your clients, your business and your leadership are going to grow exponentially. That speaks to the power of prioritization. I believe most people don't prioritize well, so they end up spending 80 percent of the time on the bottom 80 percent, and they never get anywhere.

Delegation

Prioritizing means knowing what that top 20 percent is so that you can build a system. I took a class years ago in leadership management in which they addressed delegating tasks. A leader or manager can't possibly complete every task for their business all on their own; they need a team working with them. And this means letting go of some tasks they would normally do to allow someone else on the team to complete them. This is called delegating. However, a few things must happen first in order to delegate effectively.

How to Delegate Tasks Effectively:

1. Be assured of a team member's completion of a task

2. Decipher effective resources and time to complete a task

3. Communicate well

Let's unpack each of these in more detail. When you are delegating a task to one of your team members, you must have confidence they can complete it. First, ask yourself if the job can be done (even 80 percent of it) by someone else as well as you could do it. Now, there will be some tasks as a business owner that you cannot delegate because you will own them. In fact, I heard this terminology recently used that the president has nondelegable tasks because there are some things that you must do as a business owner or a manager that shouldn't be delegated to anyone else (and maybe cannot be delegated to anyone else). You must ask yourself, can this task be delegated, and can someone do that task as well as I can?

Secondly, make sure whoever you're delegating tasks to has the resources and time to handle those tasks. While as managers and business owners we're thinking about delegating tasks and removing things from our plate, we must consider what we're putting on other people's plates. Do they have the time, the wherewithal, or the resources to take on additional tasks?

Most of the time when I delegate a task to someone in my office, they welcome the additional responsibility. But it's also important as their leader that I provide an environment that fos-

ters honesty and respect where it is okay for my team to honestly tell me if they are not able to complete a task because they do not have the time, the resources, or the skills. This helps to create a culture of openness and communication, and it will build your confidence in delegating tasks effectively in the future.

The third important step in delegating is **communicating your task** well. As the leader of your team, you must be able to clear, concise, and effective in communicating your needs for a task, which applies to the individual to which you are assigning the work as well as the others on your team. Here's a mistake that I've made, and I've seen others make it as well. Essentially, it happens when a business owner or an executive delegates a task to someone, and no one else knows about it but that individual, so when they go to perform that task or take care of that responsibility, they run into a roadblock because no one else knew that they had the ownership for that task. It's important to communicate that to whoever is involved and needs to know that a particular task has been delegated.

Another essential factor of delegating tasks well is **evaluation**. After you've delegated something, you're going to want to evaluate the task and the individual you've delegated it to. This ensures that the task is getting done and the feedback loop is working properly. When you've delegated a task to someone on your team, you must decide when you will check back with him or her to hear feedback about the task. Will it be done in a week, two weeks, or once a month? You may be asking yourself, "What is the feedback loop?"

Well, years ago, one of my executives gave me some advice: Trust but verify. I've found this advice to be very important. Regardless of how well you know a colleague you've assigned a task to, it's important to trust but verify. In some cases—depending on the individual—the trust may be there already, so the frequency of verifying may be infrequent. Whereas with someone new you're delegating a task to, you may need to check, or validate, the progress of a particular task more frequently.

I read once that it's easier to loosen the rope than it is to tighten the rope. This concept is necessary when it comes to delegation. Once you delegate a task to someone, it's important, depending on the individual, that you are following up regularly before you loosen the rope and let them do whatever they want to do and just give you the results when the project is done. The problem with doing the latter and not the former is that if you don't follow up or verify, you could find out that they started off incorrectly.

What I've learned about delegating is that, although as business owners we want to believe that we can handle every job in our organization better than most people, it is usually not true. Sometimes when we delegate a task, we are surprised how someone performs that task better than we ever imagined. That really helps me as a leader to feel more comfortable delegating because I cannot wait to see what someone does with something that I've been doing for years when they put their spin and experience on it. Oftentimes, it becomes something much better than I ever anticipated. Delegation is directly linked to prioritizing in that it frees up your time to do more and allows you to grow your business.

Efficiency is not going to happen unless you prioritize! Yet, you must also remember that prioritizing does not actually increase the time in your day or week; it just enables you to capture that time and use it more efficiently. Any business owner can use this formula to understand their priorities, build a system, delegate to their team, get their inbox to zero, and find ways to gain

20 to 30 percent more time every week, allowing them to focus on the top 20 percent of opportunities out there to grow their business. This is how you will create a win-win environment.

HEDGEHOG HINTS:

❶ Identify how you use the hours in your day.

❷ Think about how you prioritize your day.

❸ Determine how you measure a successful day.

Chapter 5:

Win/Win

> "I am not bound to win, but I am bound to be true. I am not bound to succeed, but I am bound to live up to what light I have."
>
> ~Abraham Lincoln

Drive-thru restaurants, twist-off bottle tops, voice-activated cell phones, Apple products ... the list could quite possibly go on and on. These items are all things that both the creator and the consumer can enjoy—creating a win-win situation for them both. The phrase win-win is not a new one, as it's been used and heard for centuries to describe a negotiating situation by which cooperation or participation leads to all individuals benefiting.

But what kind of benefit is received?

A few years ago, not long after losing two of my biggest clients, something happened to us that most small business owners don't plan for: a reduction in workforce. In my world, it is called a RIF (reduction in force). I had been part of many RIFs in corporate America, but I never had the full responsibility of managing this most difficult, heart-wrenching process as a business owner before. When I was in corporate America, a RIF usually began when the senior executives would begin preparing the next level executives/managers for what was to come. We would begin doing what is called "stack ranking" to determine who on our teams would go or stay. However, as a business owner, the buck stops with you. I mentally prepared myself and began sharing with my team the possibility of having to make cuts in staff based on our client portfolio if we lost some of our large clients. Because of my performance and our team's performance, I was confident that we were always going to be okay.

It was a big surprise to me when I got a call and an email from my largest client three years ago, and they mentioned that they were going to internalize their business. Nevertheless, I had to get my team prepared for a loss—a loss of 550 properties. Eventually, I ended up losing over 50 percent of my team as a result.

Shortly thereafter, another sizable investor who had 210 properties approached me. Although it was not going to make up for the 550 properties we had previously lost from our two biggest clients, it was still exciting to entertain another large investor. The investor was a local client, and he had been managing his own portfolio. Cassandra and I approached every negotiation with the goal of a win-win. A win-win is when both parties feel that they have won, that they got what they wanted or close to what they wanted in the deal. Some say that a win-win is a compromise, but it's more than just settling for something in a negotiation. Getting a win-win sometimes means that each side must give up something in order to get to that win-win, but it's not necessarily settling for less than what you desire. The end result that most people don't consider is a win-win or no deal. No deal is a situation where both sides agree to a "no deal" because there is not a real win-win solution. In some cases, the no deal is the best option. (We will discuss this option later in this chapter.)

Not Always a Win-Win

In a win-win, ideally, both parties win. However, there are some deals that end up in what is called a lose-win or a win-lose, which happens when one side feels that they're losing in the deal, and the other side feels like they're winning or have won. It's important to note that negotiating is not always a zero-sum game, which is a situation where a gain is offset by an equal loss on the other side. After meeting with this potentially large client with 210 properties for two to three weeks, it seemed like he knew a lot about my company because he had done his research. I was impressed and didn't mind his detailed knowledge of my company because we were desperate to close the deal with him.

One of the first things that I do when I meet with any client, particularly a large client, is ask for a sample of the portfolio of properties that they wanted us to manage. We like to drive by the properties and find out where they're located, the community they are in, and the distance from our office to each property. I was shocked when we got the list of the sample properties because they were in very economically challenged areas that I would consider to be high-crime areas.

This raised a huge red flag for me. When we worked the numbers, this deal would have brought about $20,000 a month in additional revenue to our business, which would have been a huge boost after losing over 550 properties. We were excited that we could potentially win this deal because every sign that this person gave us told us that they wanted us to manage their properties. But the red flag was still there in the back of my mind about the condition and the location of those potential properties. Prior to our final negotiations, Cassandra and I took the 30-minute drive to their office, along with one of our property managers. We strategized the entire way there about who would manage the portfolio, how many additional staff we would need, who would provide back-office support, how we were going to integrate this portfolio into our existing business, and so on. We were still anticipating landing this contract, yet we still had doubts in the back of our minds.

During our business meeting, we talked about the fees and came to a mutual agreement. Ironically, the client didn't negotiate the fees down, which was great for us; however, the red flag was at the back of my mind about the condition and location of those properties that we saw. I said to him during the meeting, "Although we want a win-win, I want to make sure that we discuss what that means." I said this because we didn't feel comfortable with just the sample of properties we had seen. Then I said to him, "The decision for us is this: It comes down to a safety situation. If I don't feel comfortable sending my own wife or any other person on my team to check on these properties for inspection or to post a notice on the door during the day, then we may have a problem." My apprehensions also came from knowing that 75 percent of my staff are women, and I was concerned for them.

He was puzzled that we had a problem with the properties. I said to him, "Well, we may not be able to manage those properties if the rest of the portfolio is of the same caliber as the sample that we saw." He then said, "I would never send my wife to those properties." We were shocked by his response. It seems he had given us the best of his portfolio to see. The other properties that he hadn't shared with us were apparently in even worse locations. In other words, he would never send his wife to those properties because he felt they were unsafe, which was the same feeling I had about them.

That was when I realized that although we were fighting for a win-win, in that case we made a conscious decision that we were going to walk away with no deal. When I think about what that portfolio would have done to our business in terms of how it would have negatively impacted us, I'm glad that we walked away. While the revenue would have been great, it would have changed the makeup of our office, the culture of our office, and how we do business, not to mention how other investors would view us in the marketplace in the future. Therefore, in this instance, no deal was the best option.

Committed to Your Values

Priorities are the values that drive your company. When you create and serve a client, the by-product of that relationship is a profit. But if your goal is just to chase after money through deals, even if they impact you or your company negatively, you must revisit your values.

One of our solid foundational principles is prioritizing. When your priority is not simply money, it makes it easier to make decisions, especially ones that can result in a no deal. I can tell you this, 70 percent or more of my colleagues in this same business would have taken that deal. I know that for a fact because when

I shared what happened with some of them, many of them were shocked and questioned why I didn't take the deal or ask for more money. Some also suggested solutions, like hiring a male-only staff to carry a weapon of sorts when visiting those properties in high-crime areas. But you know what? Our values and foundational principles would not allow us to cannibalize our business model and culture for the sake of money.

All would agree that the goal of negotiation is a win-win situation. That is certainly the best result. However, as my previous example with the potential property deal showed, not all deals will result in a win-win, and not all win-win results are positive ones either.

We've talked about negotiating win-win deals and no-deal situations, but there is another type of scenario called lose-win or win-lose. In 2012, right before we moved to South Florida, our Orlando office had about 450 units under management. We received a referral from one of our vendors to manage a 64-unit apartment for a prospective client. We spoke to them and negotiated for three months. Finally, when they closed on the property, they selected us, and we agreed to manage this property just outside of Orlando in a city called Titusville. This was a big win for us because this was the biggest single client deal that we had to date. We wanted to do everything that we could to make this a win-win. We negotiated the fees and conducted a break-even analysis between the client and ourselves.

The break-even analysis is simple: We determine at what point we are going to break even from this deal and start seeing some profits. Well, we did the math, and according to our calculations, we needed to have 75 percent occupancy in order to make any money. Therefore, we needed to have 48 units rented before we could start seeing a profit from this deal. Guess what? After

signing on to manage this property, we never got to 75 percent occupancy. The closest we got was 60 percent. Now, that was a challenge because we could see that, but we kept working to try to make it happen and get to that 75 percent occupancy mark. Unfortunately, it never happened. So, we began doing some more competitive analysis around the area. We looked again at the occupancy level of our competitors and learned that no one was getting over 60 percent occupancy. In other words, we were right in line with the best of our competitors in that small market.

That was a downer because the data we had gotten before stated otherwise. The fact was that we did not do enough due diligence. For four months, we tried to get to 75 percent occupancy, but we were losing money, and we knew it was going to be hard, or almost impossible, to get to that number. We began talking about possibly canceling the deal, because no one wants to be in business to lose money. And we wanted to do the right thing by our client, so we began having conversations with them about our options. Eventually, we found out from them that they were considering selling the entire apartment complex.

Now, for us, that was exciting because we did not have to terminate the agreement. You never want to terminate an agreement without a good reason when there is a great business relationship because we failed to do the right thing, and our analysis gave us the wrong data. We decided we were going to keep managing for them until they sold the apartment complex. This was a decision that I made to honor our agreement and continue managing it for them, even though we knew we were losing money, so this situation was a lose-win for us. But there's more.

It ended up turning into a win-win. One month before the apartment complex was sold, we were approached by our biggest client to date. This client, however, had one stipulation and that was that we had to have at least 500 units under management. This original "lose-win" deal turned out to be a win because that deal put us over the 500 mark, and we were able to win the largest client in our history. Under this client, our company would manage 1,200 properties simply because we stuck in there long enough, honored our commitment, and decided to keep managing the property before it was sold.

Operating on priorities and honest principles helps you make good decisions, both personally and professionally. There's no guarantee this would have turned out to be a win-win situation for my company. Even if it hadn't, we chose to stick by our principles. And we were able to sleep well at night having our integrity in place.

John Maxwell often says, "Sometimes you win, sometimes you learn." In this case we did not win with that initial deal, but we learned how to go back and communicate properly, and that lesson served us well.

Achieving a win-win doesn't always mean that it's a win-win right up front. You may have to go back to the negotiating table to get the optimum win-win. After the 64-unit deal that delivered us our largest client of 1,200 properties, we realized the company did not have many initial properties. In our haste to land this deal and because we knew they were going to purchase over 1,000 properties, we gave them a deep, deep, deep discount.

Let me explain further. In my industry, we typically charge a leasing fee to lease a property. Since we knew the volume that this company was going to give us in terms of properties to manage, we accepted a deal far less than the market average in terms of leasing fees, giving them a major discount. After managing the properties for them for close to five months, we quickly realized one thing: The discount was too deep, and we were struggling to

meet our profit margins. Although we were not losing money at the time, it was really taking a toll on my team.

I'll give you an example. When we leased the property for this client, they paid my company a leasing fee. Now if we were leasing the properties ourselves, that fee could be used to pay the commission of my team along with other fees that we charge our client. The problem in this South Florida market was that 90 percent of the properties we listed on the market were co-brokered with other outside agents. So, for example, if we listed a property on the MLS, the multiple listing system, other agents would find that property and contact us and say, "I have a tenant who's interested in this property." For that tenant referral, those agents expected a co-brokerage fee. Because 90 percent of the properties we rented in that market were co-brokered, we were losing, and our agents were losing on the front end.

The problem was, we did not do enough due diligence—a lesson we've since learned. We projected that we were going to rent 90 percent with in-house agents, and only 10 percent of them were going to be co-brokered with another outside agent, but the reverse happened. Ninety percent of the properties we listed on the market were being found on the MLS by other agents, and they were finding tenants and referring those tenants to us. Although overall, we weren't losing money because we were charging them a management fee and not just a leasing fee, we weren't getting anything on the front end.

In this particular case, although it was a win-lose initially, it turned out to be a win-win situation. Thankfully, because we were in constant communication with the client, we went back to the negotiating table with them, explained to them that we needed more incentive for the in-house property manager or realtor on my team to try to rent these homes faster. If they're

Win/Win

getting nothing, they'll place the property on the market and handle everything else, but leasing would not be their top priority. My experience in sales as a regional sales manager for Sprint taught me that when you're devising a commission-based plan, what drives performance is a commission on sales deals. Since the opposite of what we projected actually happened, my entire planning of how our people were going to get paid a commission wasn't achieved either.

After two or three weeks of negotiating with the client, we convinced them that if we were able to pay my in-house team the proper commission on leasing a home, as well as the outside agent who would refer a tenant to us, it would increase the leasing rate of these properties, allowing fewer properties to remain on the market. This decision had to go up to the executives of the company and its investors. After two to three weeks of negotiating, they agreed that this was a win-win for all of us, with incentives for both the inside agent as well as the outside agent.

This time, a win-win meant going back to the negotiating table and communicating our needs effectively. Sometimes, as a leader, you have to be willing to humble yourself and go back to your client to negotiate a better deal that is in the best interest of all your stakeholders. Our number one stakeholders are our employees, but our other important stakeholders are our clients. A win-win ensures that both sides get what they want. In this situation, my client bought into the idea that we would increase our leasing rate if the proper commission was paid, and they agreed. It took some negotiating to improve the condition of what we had initially agreed to for it to turn into a win-win situation. As a result, we were able to deliver the outcome they wanted.

I close with a quote from someone I consider to be one of the greats in entrepreneurship. Regarding a win-win situation,

Stephen Covey once said, "Win-win ... is a balancing act between courage and consideration. To go for win-win, you not only have to be empathic, but you also have to be confident. You not only have to be considerate and sensitive, but you also have to be brave. To do that—to achieve that balance between courage and consideration—is the essence of real maturity and is fundamental to a win-win."

HEDGEHOG HINTS:

How can you create a win/win situation in your negotiations?

❶ Look to Stephen Covey's words, "Seek first to understand then to be understood."

❷ Go into every negation with your goal in mind and with an open mind.

Chapter 6:

Active Listening

> *"Judge a man by his questions rather than by his answers."*
>
> ~ Voltaire

Communicating effectively is first and foremost about listening—not simply any kind of listening, but active listening. Active listening is not taught in school. We are all taught the communication skill of how to talk. However, I haven't known anyone who took a class on listening.

Active listening is more about the other person and less about yourself. When you really listen to people, you get key information that can literally solve any problem, personally or professionally. Some people would say that active listening is more about the delivery of the communicator than anything else. It's all in the way things are said. The way we listen to each other is paramount. If you're not listening with an open mind and an open heart, and you have an agenda or if you're already formulating your response or getting defensive even before you fully understand what's being spoken to you, then your listening is skewed and restricted. This limits your ability to communicate effectively as well.

Consultative Approach

When I first started out in sales, I remember being a very hungry, aggressive, and persistent salesperson because I was so eager to get my name out there and land the deal. So, when you have an opportunity to meet someone face-to-face and sell to them, you tend to want to give it everything you've got. You launch an arsenal of all the benefits for what you have to offer and why it would be to their advantage to work with you. However, the opposite happens. You don't end up making the sale, but instead, you make a lasting negative impression of yourself on that potential client. Essentially, you turn people off. I was passionate and excited, but at the end of the day, I wasn't getting the deal done. My solution was to attend a business workshop, and it absolutely, positively changed my whole approach to sales. Through it, I learned a sales technique that is called the consultative approach. This approach has become the holy grail of business, and I teach it to every one of my salespeople.

A lot of times, people in sales make the mistake of misusing the opportunity they have when someone is in front of them giving them more than 60 seconds of their undivided attention, and they load their verbal gun and start shooting their sales bullets without necessarily having the best aim. As a result, they just end up shooting in all different directions, but not hitting a target. I was one of these sales professionals.

I wanted to learn better sales techniques, so I attended a workshop. There, they trained us in the **consultative approach: He who asks the questions controls the conversation**. The premise behind the consultative approach is to ask questions to determine the main point and to drill down on the issue. Once you identify the issues, then you can drill down your pitch to your client. That's when the light bulb went off for me, and I immediately understood. The way the workshop was presented made me think of an experience at the doctor's office.

If you envision the process of going to the doctor, here's what happens. When you visit the doctor's office, your typical experience involves walking into the office where you're handed a clipboard with a list of probing questions. Sometimes the questions themselves even get you to ask, "Why am I really here?" It drills it down for you and helps you hone in on your exact personal issue. Sometimes, even the questions are guided, and they're giving you suggestions of what the options of the symptoms are. For example, are you experiencing a fever? Is it stomach pain? Have you had a previous diagnosis or familial history? These questions are geared to pinpoint the origin of the problem.

> **Listen to your clients and listen to your team.**

It would be odd if you walked into a doctor's office and suddenly the doctor said, "Okay, so this is what you have, and here's a prescription for it. And we're going to give you this pain med." At that point, you would be suspicious or skeptical of the diagnosis that you're receiving. Because how could the doctor give you a prescription or a diagnosis and not first ask one question about how you feel, what's bothering you, what's concerning you, or what caused you to come to the office in the first place? And this is the mistake that many people in sales make. People do this in their business as well. Not listening well can result in misdiagnoses and incorrect remedies or solutions.

Having learned from my mistakes, I now teach better techniques to every single one of my salespeople. With active listening, what you want to do is ask the question(s) and then stop speaking so you can listen well. The more you listen, the more clues you'll find. As you let the client speak, you'll begin to ask more probing questions to get to the heart of the matter and learn how to solve their problem effectively. Moreover, you'll be able to make the sale and land your deal effectively. If you really listen to people and understand their issues, you've got a captive audience, and they're willing to hear about how you can help them.

Do you know what's interesting about that approach? Just by virtue of somebody addressing those issues, your potential client will feel better because someone took the time to listen intently and offer you some reprieve. People want to be heard and understood, and if you're not practicing active listening, then the people you encounter won't feel understood. Ultimately, people are just looking for a solution to their problems, and you can be the solution—or in the least provide them with a solution—by actively listening.

First, remember to ask the right questions. You may not be an expert in how to solve their particular business problem, but because you are willing to ask pointed questions to try to get at something, you'll end up discovering so much more. Questions and active listening provide clarification. If you're taking the initiative and you're asking the right questions, then you're actively listening; you're going to find a solution to whatever you're encountering, and you're going to come up with a better solution.

Recognizing the Value of Your Team

Maybe you've been in an organization where a new policy, new system, or a new piece of equipment is being presented, and no one took the time to talk to the people that are going to be implementing or using this new product or service in order to form their decision for implementing it. This is a mistake. It's important to listen to the people that report to you. In our business, for example, every year we do a **SWOT (Strengths, Weaknesses, Opportunities, and Threats) Analysis** where the team gets together and talks about what's happening in our industry—the strength and weaknesses, the opportunities, and threats in our business. The SWOT analysis tool is part of a larger business process called a situational analysis, but SWOT is the most commonly used evaluation method when planning or evaluating a business. We do a SWOT analysis every year, and we engage everyone—from the receptionist to the runner and the property managers to the managers (and anyone involved in the process). The feedback that we get year after year is that everyone gets to voice their opinion and see a change happen or watch how some of their ideas affect change.

One of the things that would come up when we received feedback was that our team really wanted a consistent forum to communicate all their ideas or the things that they observed. We wanted to try to come up with a way to create that opportunity for our team members to share their ideas.

We attended a conference and ran into a gentleman that was talking about just how he did that with a tool called Officevibe. So, we did some research and found more information about it before we decided to go ahead and utilize Officevibe in our own offices. Officevibe is a service that sends a survey periodically throughout the week to employees. All the survey questions are created by Officevibe and not by our office. Moreover, employees can complete the survey anonymously, providing an opportunity for them to share their opinion honestly. We believe this process is so brilliant because you get a real-time pulse on what's happening in your office and how your team is affected by how you run your business. You get a chance to hear the voices of the people. This proactive approach is the driving force behind active listening. You're proactively listening so that you can come up with a solution to help prevent, resolve, or promote. We have four offices, and we don't get an opportunity to interface with our people on a regular basis. Yet, we still want to have an influence on our culture, and we still want to have a pulse on what's happening. It's been a very, very important tool for us, but I'm sure other tools or approaches can be just a valuable.

> **Listen to your clients, listen to your prospects, and also listen to your team.**

One option is that you could conduct face-to-face meetings where managers would meet directly with employees to get a pulse on what's happening in the day to day and how change can be affected. Or you could do what's known as a skip level; if you're a Senior Manager, you could meet with the employees directly because sometimes the managers may not give you a real view of what's happening. This provides a way for business owners to stay in touch with what's happening in their business and work on providing a fix, if necessary.

Active listening also means taking initiative. If your employees take the time to fill out a weekly survey and you don't take action, they will likely read that as you either not caring or just giving up on them. If your goal is to see your business and employees thrive, then you must actively listen and take action.

Our employees know that we care because they voice their opinion and we respond. We may not have an immediate solution or resolve, but we take action in whatever way we can. Maybe someone wants a raise. We may not be able to give that to them, but sometimes it just feels good to know that your boss is actually listening and responding to you and that they care.

Now here's an interesting feature about the Officevibe survey. Once a month an email is sent out to each employee to remind him or her to complete their survey that week. If an employee has not responded in a while because they are out of the office or on vacation, then the software will send out a follow-up email saying, "Hey. We haven't heard from you in [specified number] weeks. We'd love your feedback. Your feedback is valuable to the leaders, so please be sure to respond to the survey." An email like this not only encourages the reader to complete their survey, but it also reassures them that they have an active voice in the company. When you are actively following up with people, they know they matter. Part of the culture we are building in our company is that we care.

Copreneurs

Active listening is not something we only practice in a business setting. Cassandra and I are not only partners in business but also partners in life, so actively listening to each other extends beyond the office. I like to call our relationship one of copreneurs—a new term we've adopted—which labels and explains the symbiotic relationship between us as a husband and wife who are also partners in business. Cassandra and I work together, and we live together. I get to spend 90 percent of my time with Cassandra throughout the day because we're never too far from each other.

Copreneurs is new terminology that you won't likely find in Webster's Dictionary. At least not yet, but it does have a meaning. It explains the balance of understanding each other in each form of your relationship—both business and personal. Actively listening to your partner from the business perspective as well as the personal perspective creates a deeper relationship for the two of you.

I remember vividly having conversations with Cassandra on many occasions where she would begin talking to me about a problem, and before she could finish telling me the story, I would start solving the problem or telling her what she should do. I wasn't actively listening; instead, I was taking over the conversation. Truthfully, she just wanted to share with me what happened to her at work that day. So, she would look at me and say, "I don't need you to solve the problem. I just need you to listen." As a man and a husband, I automatically want to solve all her problems without actually listening well. However, Cassandra is really great at listening, so she is teaching me how to be a better listener. I've learned from her that sometimes people are talking to you not so you can solve their problem, but so that you can just listen to them.

V-A-L-U-E

I've created an acronym that I believe represents active listening. The acronym is VALUE: V-A-L-U-E, and I call these the five steps for active listening:

- **V–Value others**. A man that I highly respect, Stephen Covey, once said, "What's important to someone should be as important to you as that person is to you."

- **A–Acknowledge**. Acknowledge the person speaking to you for sharing something that is important to them. So, start with an acknowledgment like a thank you. For example, if it's a client, say, "Thank you for calling, and thank you for telling me about what you're looking for." When you acknowledge someone, they feel valued.

- **L–Listen sincerely**. Instead of listening to respond, listen so you can really understand. This is what it means to listen sincerely.

- **U–Use questions** for clarifications. Remember, it's not about getting the right answers; it's about asking the right questions. When you're talking to a client, it's important to ask open-ended questions to get to the root of the issue.

- **E–End it**–Lastly, for active listening to take place, you must end it. Be sure to end your conversation with, "How can I help?" Many times, we gain clients not because we're smarter than our competitors but because we ask that simple question, "How can I help?"

HEDGEHOG HINTS:

❶ People may not remember what you say, but they will remember how you made them feel.

❷ Communication is more about listening than speaking.

Active Listening

Chapter 7:

Synergy

"I have found no greater satisfaction than achieving success through honest dealing and strict adherence to the view that, for you to gain, those you deal with should gain as well."

~Alan Greenspan

I was 19 years old when I was introduced to Stephen Covey and the word synergy. I don't know if I had ever heard of it before or maybe never paid attention to it, but this is how he defines synergy:

> "Synergy is where the whole is greater than the sum of its parts. Synergy takes place when two or more people produce more together than the sum of what they can do ... have produced separately."

Back in the early 2000s, as a young professional, I worked in the telecom industry. This industry was notorious for mergers and acquisitions. During that time, many companies began using the word synergy when asked why so many mergers and acquisitions were taking place. The response was usually something to this effect: *We are merging or going through an acquisition because there will be great synergy between the two companies.* That was the likely response you would get from the executives when you asked, "Why are you merging?" Everyone in the industry got used to these synergistic mergers. Since these companies were merging and acquiring each other all the time, one day your fiercest competitor could become your coworker.

In a synergistic relationship, the two business relationships can get more done together than they could separately. In essence, synergy in business is a goal to strive toward when success is what you want to achieve. It is two companies working together as one.

In the business world, synergies are created in a few ways:

- Mergers
- Organizational restructuring
- Creating work groups/teams

Mergers are probably the most popular and talked about when it comes to synergy. There have been successful business mergers (and some unsuccessful ones as well). The successful ones are the triggers or catalysts for other companies to consider synergy for themselves through mergers.

In 2006, Disney and Pixar merged their companies, resulting in one of the largest and most successful mergers in the history of the industry. The quality of animated/children's programming was taken to a whole new level of excellence and sales. Not to mention that the high-playing stakeholders, like the late Steve Jobs and executives at Disney, saw their net worth increase. Another successful company merger was between Sirius and XM satellite radio, where it was said that these two companies were smart to "join forces in a down market."[1] Ultimately, the synergy that resulted from these mergers produced a successful and a win-win result for everyone involved: the companies themselves, their executives, and their employees.

Companies often merge to capitalize on a particular resource or market that they had not (or could not have) tapped into on their own. For example, East Coast companies may be interested in merging with companies that have operations based on the West Coast in order to expand their national footprint. Others may merge because one company has technology or resources that can help other people, other companies, or vice versa. In other words, companies want to merge to create this synergistic acquisition to present themselves as marketable alongside and competitive with the larger players in the industry.

When There Is No Synergy

On the other hand, many of these supposed synergistic acquisitions or mergers can prove unsuccessful. Even worse, some of these companies end up worse off after the merger than they were before the merger. I've seen this happen with many companies. To understand why this happens, one must look at how synergy is created. Now, I'm very passionate about sports, and I've mentioned this a few times already. Since I'm a sports fan, particularly

---

[1] CNBC Online; https://www.cnbc.com/2009/12/29/Top-10-Best-(and-Worst)-Mergers-of-All-Time.html?slide=4

basketball, I often try to seek similarities from my beloved sport as it relates to business.

Creating team synergy in sports is a method that has been used for centuries. As a fan, I watched teams and franchises acquire players, and often I wondered why because I didn't often see the synergy of how it was going to work. To create synergy, you must first have a strategy for the key pieces that you're looking to integrate. You must know how partnering with other groups or players will help increase efficiency so that you and your business can ultimately grow and thrive. For example, I've watched a lot of teams acquire the so-called big-name players or stars, paying them astronomical amounts of money. But sometimes that star player does not end up integrating well with the team or the culture of the new franchise. Therefore, talent and resources alone are not enough to create synergy. (This makes me think of one of my favorite authors, John Maxwell, who wrote a book titled *Talent is Never Enough*.)

Synergy happens when all the pieces complement each other, when there's a clear understanding of roles and, most importantly, when the partnering will benefit the company's vision and mission. Still, some mergers take advantage of what we call economies of scale. Economies of scale happen when proportionate cost savings are gained by increased levels of production. This usually is done by removing redundancies between business units and combining groups while increasing efficiency. This is one of the main goals for synergy—part of economies of scale.

The interesting thing is that many of these synergistic mergers have worked really well, and some of these companies that merged are still thriving today.

One of the most dominating NBA players was Shaquille O'Neil. I'm sure you know his name because you couldn't have been around in the 1990s or 2000s and not know who Shaq was. He was Orlando's No. 1 draft pick, I believe, in 1992. And I happened to live in Orlando at the time; I started school in Orlando in 1994. He played for Orlando for years until he was recruited by the Los Angeles Lakers to go to a bigger market. Now, I'm not promoting Shaq, but what I want to point out is that Shaq understood his role, his talents, and his skill set, and he tried to find teams that needed his talents. He wanted to find a team that would surround him with complementary players with complementary skills in order to create synergy. Now, his stay in LA was rocky because while the players—in particular, the great Kobe Bryant—complemented Shaq's skills, they didn't always have synergy off the court, and it was public knowledge that they did not get along. But on the court, they were unstoppable! They ended up winning three NBA championships, showing it as a great example of synergy on the court. Shaq made another bold move a few years later when he was acquired by Miami, and this acquisition created great synergy. He partnered with a young talent by the name of Dwayne Wade, and this partnership also led to an NBA championship. I think you can always look to sports to see the philosophy of something as complicated as a synergistic merger and how it plays out in the real world.

Building Our Team

Back in 2014, Cassandra and I wanted to open our third office. We had opened two offices in the three years before, and the expansion of the second office had taken a huge toll on our family. However, we knew we needed some help. Just to give a quick example: I lived in Orlando, and I opened an office in South Florida, which is four hours away. For six months, I was driving back and forth to those two cities by myself twice a week.

Cassandra and the kids stayed in the house in Orlando while I continued to take the exhaustive drive back and forth to South Florida to our second office. I knew that wanting to open a third office meant that we couldn't continue to keep up this lifestyle, and we certainly couldn't do it alone.

We evaluated why we were in business in the first place. The expansion did not make sense from a sacrifice perspective. The only way we could do it was to have synergy with others who were also interested in the vision of opening an office in North Florida. In other words, we needed to partner with someone or with a company whose talent and way of doing business complemented our style and our skill. Fortunately, we didn't have to look too far.

One of my best property managers is Paula Givler, who I met back in my days at telecom. She was always phenomenal in sales and business development. I quickly found out when she began working for me in Orlando that she was interested in running her own real estate property management office. The problem was she didn't have the resources to do it alone. While she did not have the resources and skills, we knew that she was fantastic at business development, and she could close business like no one else. She's the type of person that if you put her in a conference room or a networking event with 100 people, by the end of that event, everyone in that room would know who she was. They would all begin inviting her to birthday parties and weddings, which happens all the time. In fact, next week she's going to someone's wedding. She has the ability to bring people into her fold; they trust her, and they want to share business with her. So, we knew that even though she didn't have the resources, she had the talent to grow the business. She became one of our synergy contenders.

More people also approached us; one was a good friend of mine named Darryl Gichia-Broussard. He and his wife Njeri Gichia-Broussard were interested in partnering with us as well. Darryl and I went to school together at UCF back in the '90s. He and I both started off as engineering students, but I left that program to focus on a business degree because that was more my calling. He stayed and continued on as an engineer and ended up working for NASA for 14 years, while I worked for the telecom industry for 14 years.

Darryl is extremely analytical because of his experience as a mechanical engineer. His partnership with us would be a tremendous synergistic relationship, because what I lack in analytical prowess, Darryl would fill in. I'm more of a leadership kind of person—leadership development and strategy. But I knew that having him on the team would be a benefit to me. His wife was also a complement to our business because of her frugality; she would watch the financials like a hawk. We knew that having those two people on our team, along with Paula Givler, would be the exact merger our company needed.

To cap it off, we had another option in a friend and employee by the name of Reshard Battle. I met him while I was a student at UCF, and he was my first tenant when I bought my first house while I was still a student there. Reshard graduated with a degree in marketing and showed some interest in a partnership with us. His attention to detail would be a great asset to our company. Cassandra and I knew that we could not operate this business and all its offices on our own. Each of these individuals would add value to our team.

And then there's Cassandra, my best partner of all, the one I have the best synergistic relationship with. She is the glue that makes it all work. People say that I'm very passionate, and it can be intimidating. Cassandra softens me. She makes me palatable, because sometimes I might scare people with my passion. But Cassandra is a great communicator, which is evidenced in all her relationships. For example, when building our business, I'm going to care a lot about the vision and team development, while she cares more about the process. And she always says that you've got to make sure you fall in love with the process.

So, we went ahead and put together that team of people to open our third office, because we knew we couldn't do it alone. Synergy is why we were successful. When we decided to expand our business into the North Florida market and take on a few investors, we knew that we wanted to create a synergistic team. We acknowledged that we wanted to partner with a few individuals who shared in our vision. The intention was to create a diverse team whose members had a winning attitude.

As a result of this synergistic team, the Jacksonville office has been one of the fastest-growing All County Property Management offices ever. It has broken all the sales records of any other office (including my first two offices), and all the partners are extremely excited about the future of that office.

Creating Synergy

To create synergy, first you need to have a **mutually agreed-upon goal and vision**, and as the leader for that office, I wanted to set the stage for it. The very first thing I wanted to ask the team was, "What do you want out of this office?" And I wanted to make sure that together we mutually agreed upon the vision for the office.

Secondly, you have to **value diversity**. Stephen Covey mentioned in his book that strength lies in differences, not simi-

larities, and you must buy into that because too often we find business people who want to partner with people who look like them, talk like them, sound like them, and even dress like them. Yet, the strength of a company, particularly a company that is creating synergy through a merger, is always in their ability to embrace differences and not similarities.

Thirdly, you must have a **win-win attitude**. Obviously, we wrote a whole chapter on win-win, but your attitude has to be pointed toward win-win every time in order to have a synergistic approach. You may have to give up something to get a win-win, but that must be the attitude of the group.

Next, you must **understand each player**. What I mean by that is you must evaluate and understand the skill level of everyone on the team and what they bring, so you can see if they are complementary to each other. Let's go back to the example of Shaq as one of the most dominating players in the 1990s and the early 2000s. If you had five Shaq's on one team, you would not win many games if each player on the team didn't complement each other. The reason is simple; an organization or team must have diversity in skill set and talent to be great (or even good).

And last but not least, always **seek a third alternative**. Even though I'm the leader for my office, I must make sure that I also work on my listening skills. Cassandra is the expert in that area. However, I try to listen to the ideas that are being shared by the other partners. There are times when my ideas may not be the best, and their ideas may not be the best, but a third alternative might be the best solution in order for synergy to take place. The third alternative is usually a collaborative idea or strategy created by the group; it's *not* simply a compromise.

Synergy as Copreneurs

So how does synergy work with Cassandra and me? Well, we complement each other so well. Before Cassandra and I got together, I was single and lived alone. Whenever I cooked, my food was always bland. It was still edible, but it wasn't tasty. Then Cassandra came into my life and added more to it. To my food, she added spices. She makes everything that I do better, and I hope that I make her life better as well.

The cooking example is just one small example, but it is always true when it comes to how I do business. When I met Cassandra, I was even more passionate than I am now, but I didn't have a human aspect to me. I was really more robotic than human from a business perspective because I was so focused on results, results, results. Then, Cassandra softened me, and now I take time to listen and have that extra conversation with someone. I choose to take time to enjoy the people around me; it's not just about the results. If we take time to appreciate those around us, then we could experience the kind of results that help our business—and lives—soar exponentially.

From a partnership-leader perspective, copreneurs must have synergy in their relationship. To have great synergy, you must have people who are independent, people who can do well on their own, but who also know how to complement those around them. When you have synergy, one plus one equals three or five or 10. One plus one is not two, but one plus one could be exponentially greater than just two. Does that make sense?

You can either have oil and water—which don't fit well together and separate—or you can have a glove and a hand; though they're opposites, they fit together perfectly. That is synergy!

HEDGEHOG HINTS:

❶ The whole is greater than the sum of its parts.

❷ "Build on strengths to compensate for weaknesses."

– Stephen Covey

❸ Working together takes time but produces better long-term results.

Chapter 8:

Grow

"When you stop growing you start dying."

~Lou Holtz

Everything in life, with its makeup of atoms and cells, has an inception, which then evolves or grows into something more. When a business or company first starts off, it sets a goal to grow, and it must put certain things in place to facilitate and cultivate that growth. Standing still or staying the same in business is a surefire way for a company to crumble into extinction.

As a young, up-and-coming, 19-year-old professional, I was fortunate to have some incredible leaders who challenged me and encouraged me to grow. Honestly, I still don't know what they saw in me. What I did notice was that since I had a desire to learn everything they were teaching me, I became a quick study. I was able to understand new ideas quickly, and even more importantly, I was able to retain that knowledge and apply it in later situations.

Leadership Training

I had a manager at Sprint's Human Resource Training Department named Nancy Garrett, who enrolled me in a one-week workshop/conference called *The 7 Habits of Highly Effectively People*. I did not know who Stephen Covey was at the time. At first, I did not know what to expect; however, this workshop changed my professional life. I immersed myself in the entire week of the material they taught us.

Additionally, I went on to attend countless other conferences. I also joined the John Maxwell Maximum Impact Club. This program, created in the early 2000s by John Maxwell, was based on a monthly subscription that entitled the subscriber to a gift of monthly audio CDs. There were a series of about 20 of them, and every month you'd get a new one. I'd listen to each CD at least 10 to 20 times before I got the next one. When I was listening to that material and going through the workbook that came with it, the words would not leave my mind. Those words would be on my mind and coming out of my mouth as I would coach, develop, and build my team in the corporate world.

At the same time, I also began attending workshops and reading books by Tony Robbins. I immersed myself in leadership knowledge, going on to earn countless certifications in my industry. (I also did that back in my Sprint days as a project manager when the company sponsored me to complete a three-year Master of Science in Project Management via George Washington University.) When I was in my 20s, most of my colleagues did not want to spend an enormous amount of time learning, reading, and doing projects. But guess what? I went on to get a master's in project management, and, as a result, I was offered a higher-level project management position in the company because I had done the work.

It was also around that time that one of my managers recommended we get involved in Toastmasters. I had no idea what Toastmasters was, so she had to explain it to me. She strongly suggested it to me and challenged me to see if it would produce growth in my life and future business. The one I joined was in downtown Orlando. There were around 40 people in that chapter. We had the county tax collector, businesspeople, attorneys, and professors from the local colleges—UCF, Rollins College, and even the community college.

> **A competent team performs at a higher level than an incompetent team.**

I was not in my element in that setting yet, but I immersed myself in it. I was uncomfortable, but I firmly believe that if you're not uncomfortable, you're not growing. I put myself in the position where I was the youngest person in the sea of very, very knowledgeable executives 15 years my senior. One of the most impressive people there was the Orlando tax collector, Earl K. Wood. Every Monday night I would meet with these people, and some would give a speech—usually a five- to seven-minute speech—and get feedback from the best of the best in Central Florida. All these prominent people were pouring into me, and that for me was amazing.

The Toastmasters group met every Monday night at 7 p.m. during football season while all my friends were watching Monday Night Football.

Although there were many times I missed out on those weekly football hangouts with friends, that period in my life enabled me

Grow  101 to learn and grow more than most of my colleagues or peers. I regularly attended these meetings and always had my head in a book. It was no surprise that when I met Cassandra, I was reading a book. In fact, she wrote her number on the cover of that book. I still have that book sitting on my shelf.

Our kids even know the book because they always ask us how we met, and we've shared that story with them while showing them the book.

My point is that growth has always been a part of me.

Today, there's not a week that goes by where I don't use those same habits I learned at that workshop or talk about them in my business.

Now, as a business owner, I'm teaching other business leaders and business students some of the very same principles that I learned from my mentors. We created what is called a growth plan for every position in our company. This tool allows every employee to create a road map of courses, classes, conferences, and certifications that they will commit to as a way to continue to grow in their role and prepare themselves for the next one.

GROWTH MATRIX

Position	Transaction Desk	RE License	BNI	Toastmasters	GRI	CPS	Broker License	ABR	SRS	NARPM	CRS	Sales Training	Notary	Rent MGR	ShowMojo	MLS	Lead Simple	Chamber Memb	CFR
PM	X	X	X	X	X		X	X				X		X		X	X		X
Sr. PM	X	X	X	X	X	X	X	X	X			X		X	X	X	X	X	
GM	X	X	X	X	X	X	X	X	X	X		X		X	X	X	X	X	
Ops Spec 1														X		X	X		
Ops Spec 2		X												X	X	X	X		
Ops MGR		X	X		X				X				X	X	X	X		X	
Bookeeker		X											X	X	X	X			

Growth=Life

Growth has a lot to do with sharpening the saw, the seventh habit of highly effective people. Sharpening the saw is a competitive advantage that every professional can give himself or herself that young professionals—or even professionals in their 40s or 50s—don't often utilize. As a result, they're competing with people who are far ahead of them in terms of knowledge and experience because those people expose themselves to more information, and they are growing.

The truth is that if you're not growing, you're dying. By growing and ensuring that your team is growing as a business owner, you are increasing the overall competency of that team. A competent team performs at a higher level than an incompetent team. Ultimately, the business will thrive when you have a culture of continuous growth.

What do you need for continuous growth? Here are the top three things you can do to grow:

1. **Have a growth plan.** Do something as simple as writing down your goals or intentions for this year, this month, or this quarter to grow in your role professionally, personally, and spiritually. Cassandra and I look at that on a yearly basis, and then we break it down every month. This month Cassandra and I just completed our certification to become certified international property specialists (CIPS). Now we're certified to work with international clients, and we have been traveling internationally. This is an example of our growth. And then next month, we're both completing the GRI, the Graduate Real Estate Institute, which is essentially a master's level of real estate knowledge. When it comes to a growth plan, every leader must have one for himself or herself, but every leader must ensure their team

members have that as well. Remember, if you increase the overall competency of the team, the business will thrive.

2. **Find mentors**. Don't just find a mentor, but find mentors. You might not find only one individual but 20 people that you talk to on a regular basis, people that you look up to. I've never met some of my mentors; they're just books and authors of books that I admire. For instance, I've never met Stephen Covey, but I tell everyone he's my mentor. However, I have met John Maxwell, I'm part of the John Maxwell team, and I've learned a great deal from him. Moreover, people don't often think about this, but in order to grow, you must also mentor someone. Here's the interesting thing about the mentor-mentee relationship: Every time you get to mentor someone, you can pour knowledge into that person and help them grow while also growing yourself. The more I mentor others, the more I realize that I'm also growing in the process. Here's an example: When I went to speak at Indiana University in 2017, I did not know that I would meet a professor of real estate who is now planning to fly to South Florida to meet with me to help put together a synergistic partnership between my client and his developer in Indiana. When you mentor someone, doors open—not just for the mentee, but for the mentor. You end up building it with somebody else and getting it right back, and you both end up growing.

3. **Take initiative**. From the time I was a young man (always the youngest in the room) just starting out in the business world, I was hungry. So, I took the initiative and got the degree and training I needed. Now, I take initiative in all areas of my life. It's about personal growth first, and then it goes off to the next concen-

tric circle, which is your team and building a cultural growth through your growth plan.

I've learned many valuable lessons throughout my time as a business leader, from leadership conferences to my experiences in my company. And one thing that always holds true is this quote, coined first by business owner Frank Outlaw and then redone by Ralph Waldo Emerson:

> Watch your thoughts for they become words.
> Watch your words for they become actions.
> Watch your actions, for they become habits.
> Watch your habits for they become your character.
> Watch your character for it becomes your destiny.

Cassandra and I have a growth plan, and we attempt to convey and teach that plan to our employees and teammates so that they do it for themselves. This will allow it to have a ripple effect and continue to go out. What you plant will inevitably grow. Growth is central to all our lives if we're going to do and be more. So, carefully consider the thoughts, words, actions, habits, and character that you are planting both professionally and personally.

HEDGEHOG HINTS:

Ask yourself these questions regularly

❶ How do you want to see yourself grow?

❷ How do you want to see your business grow, and what are you doing to allow that to happen?

❸ What have you done in the last 12 months to improve personally and professionally?

❹ What have you done to help your team or those around you improve?

Grow

SECTION 2:

The Pillars

OUR VALUES

Our values serve us as a compass for our actions and describe how we do business

Chapter 9:

Integrity

"A quiet conscience makes one strong!"

~Anne Frank, The Diary of a Young Girl

Integrity should be the cornerstone of any business, and it certainly is the cornerstone of ours. If you look at our pillars—our core values—the first one is integrity. We came up with other core values that are important to us in business as well: accountability, communication, and teamwork. However, integrity was definitely the first item that we thought about relating to how we wanted to do business. Integrity is a quality, a character trait.

In a nutshell, integrity is doing the right thing(s) when no one is watching, even when it hurts. From a business owner's perspective, having a strong stance on integrity is key to cultivating a culture of integrity. In other words, if the leader is a person that stands firmly on integrity, they typically have a company, a culture, where that is a cornerstone. However, if the leader is open to laissez-faire, getting the business at all costs, no matter how you compete to kill your opponent, it will deteriorate the culture of the company.

Integrity in Action

Back in 2011, just two years after we opened our office in Orlando, we were faced with a situation in which we had to rely on this core value of integrity to make the right decision. For any property management company, the first week of the month is always filled with lots of activities, as you can imagine. It's usually the case that many tenants are moving in and rent is typically due for most of them. Our clients, the property owners that we manage properties for, expect rent to be collected and expect the rental income. At that time, we were managing between 250 to 300 properties. One of the most important things we monitor very closely in our company is delinquency. Delinquency simply refers to how much rent was not collected divided by the gross potential rent. That gives you a delinquency percentage by which, as a company, you can manage and see how well you're performing in that category.

Integrity is the quality of being honest and having strong moral principles or moral uprightness.

After the first week of October 2011, we noticed our delinquency rate was unusually high. Our delinquency rate is typically between 15 and 20 percent after the first week, which occurs because a lot of tenants do pay late, and we expect it to be in that range. But it was very surprising to us when our delinquency that month was well over 25 percent, which was higher than normal.

After we posted our normal three-day notices—notices to pay or vacate the property if you haven't paid—to tenants whose rent we hadn't received, we began hearing from many tenants that they had paid their rent, but for some odd reason we had not received their rent payment.

A total of 12 tenants had made that same claim. After further investigation, we learned that all those tenants had something in common: they had all paid with a money order. Moreover, they claimed that they had dropped the funds in our night drop box. I thought that it was all a coincidence. Why was it that all the tenants who hadn't paid claimed that they paid with money orders? That had to be a coincidence—or so we thought. We did some further investigation and learned that our drop box had been compromised. Someone had fished the money orders out of it. They didn't take the checks, only the money orders. The total was about $17,000. Regardless of the size of the business, that is a large sum of money.

At the time, we were doing alright since our business was taking a turn, and we had landed some large clients. It was an interesting month for us because we were excited that we had acquired a large client, but the loss of $17,000 really took a toll on our business and me. We continued our investigation, and upon contacting the company that these tenants claimed that they had purchased their money orders from, we learned that the money orders had been cashed—but not by our firm or any known persons. In other words, when you receive a money order, you must go to a designated retail store or a bank to cash it (and they usually require some form of ID) or deposit it in your bank account. Usually, there's a stamp that indicates who cashed the money order.

Integrity

Meanwhile, when the money order company investigated further, they found it hadn't been anyone from our company or anyone that we knew cashed the money orders. The property owners, still had not received their rental income in a little over a week. Naturally, the owners began asking questions, "Hey, what's going on? Did my tenants pay their rent?" We reached out to several sources for guidance on how to address the nonpayment issue. One source advised us to go through the normal eviction process for the tenants because, technically, we did not receive the rent from all the tenants. In order to do this, our clients, the property owners, needed to approve this. Many of them didn't have any problem with that; they knew that we didn't have the money that the tenants claimed that they paid us, although someone—not anyone in our company—had cashed the money orders. But something didn't feel right about going down that path knowing that the tenants had proof that they had purchased the money orders.

So, we reached out to our attorney at the Kelley & Grant law firm for legal counsel and explained the situation. Surprisingly, the lead attorney, Mr. Kelley, said, "I can take your money and file the eviction on the 12 tenants. The total cost for these evictions would cost you $6,000." He then said, "However, I would advise you against that." Although his firm could have made $6,000 plus additional attorney fees if the tenants contested, he said, "I can take your money, but it's not a good idea." Now, I appreciated his honesty because some law firms get a bad reputation for just taking your money regardless of whether they think you're going to win. But he advised us sincerely and to our benefit.

Once we reevaluated the options and possible course of action, we made the decision based on our core values, which we keep posted on a wall in the office. I vividly remember when Cassandra and I addressed our management team about the issue. Although it was a tough time for us, and it was quite a big decision, we relied on our core values and business standard to make a critical decision.

Integrity means making the right decision even when it hurts. In this case, we decided to take on the expense and pay the rent for those tenants who claimed that they had paid.

When we did address it with the money order company, we were only able to retrieve about half of the lost money; they could not refund us the remainder. But we made the decision prior to knowing what the outcome would be that we would recover any of those funds because integrity was our cornerstone. Contrary to the popular opinion and the advice of others in the property management business, we decided to fight the money order company ourselves on behalf of the tenants. We were told that this was not the standard way to handle things as a property management company because, typically, the tenants are responsible for fighting the money order company themselves.

Integrity, for us, proves to be the most important act as a business. When push comes to shove, rely on integrity.

Now as a company, this was one of the most significant situations for us from an integrity perspective. But I have another example of how integrity can assist you in business.

When Integrity Doesn't Make Sense

In the early years of our management company, we were approached by another potential franchisee that wanted to open an office not far from ours, about 30 minutes away. Now, if you own the rights to a particular territory and another potential franchisee comes in, they are not exactly your competitors. However, at the time, what was going through my mind and I imagine through the collective minds of the team was: *This guy's going to compete and take some of the business that we would have gotten if he wasn't there.* Well, that's what we thought.

Nonetheless, this gentleman reached out to us. And not only was he opening an office next door to us, but he also asked if I could become his mentor. He asked for my help because he said that since I was in business for a year and a half and our business was growing, he needed my help for his business growth as well. He said, "I want you to help me with navigating through the land mines of opening a business in property management: what to do, what not to do, and maybe even shadow you and do some marketing with you."

When I explained his interest and requests to our team, many of them were cynical and said, "Wait a minute. Number one, this person's going to open an office next door, which is going to cut into our potential business, but now he wants you to spend time with him to help him essentially compete?" Even though we were part of the same franchise, there was still some level of competition because we were in the same market.

Nevertheless, I did decide to meet with this gentleman and his wife to discuss the possibility of mentoring him. I spent many days meeting with him to discuss marketing, having phone meetings and in-office meetings, and assisting him with setting up his business for success.

Now, I thought that was the end of it, but he reached out to us again. He knew Cassandra had her brokerage license, and this gentleman asked, "Can you or your wife be the qualifying broker for my office since we're in the same market?" Typically, when someone asks you to be the qualifying broker, it comes at a cost, since most real estate brokers will charge to be the qualifying broker because there is some level of liability that comes with that responsibility. Cassandra, being a person of integrity, said, "Why not? And we don't even need to charge him. Just try to do what we can to help."

Again, some members of the team were not enthusiastic about our decision to mentor him. To top it off, we were also going to put Cassandra's name on his door as his qualifying broker. Nevertheless, Cassandra said, "The type of business we want to operate is a business with integrity."

This went on for two years; we continued to mentor and guide the gentleman and his company whenever he needed our help. But during those two years, Cassandra's name was still on their door as a qualifying broker, although we were not the owners of that office. It took them two years to get their licenses together and remove Cassandra's name from their door and replace it with their own.

I remember when that happened; they called us to celebrate with them. They took us out to dinner to thank us. We thought that was the end of our business relationship because we had passed the torch in a sense.

Well, we were soon surprised a year later. We had been in business for about three and a half years at that point, and our lease was up for our building and our office suite. We needed to relocate. We looked everywhere in Central Florida for the perfect office space, but we couldn't find anything. We finally found an office space located in the heart of downtown Orlando. The only problem was the downtown office space was in a noncompete territory, which meant according to our franchise agreement, the two offices that are in Orlando could not be in the same territory or zip code unless we wanted to pay a fine to the franchisor to purchase that zip code. And it was a hefty one-time fee to own that zip code because it was a prime location. The only other option that the corporate office offered was suggesting we get together with the local All County franchisee (which happened to be our old friend and mentee) and negotiate with him, and maybe we could consider doing something different.

I immediately reached out to the neighboring franchisee who I had mentored for about two years. Do you know what he said? He said, "Socrate, you know, the corporate office has already called me, and they told me the cost for this. I really want that territory, and you want it as well. It's never been sold to anyone. However, we modeled our business after you, and integrity is important to us. I'm willing to tell the corporate office that I don't mind if you move your location to that zip code. You were there to support me when I opened my office, so I want to return the favor."

Wow! We were completely shocked and excited by his kind gesture.

We reached out to the corporate office with the news, and we explained to them that he didn't want any payment for us moving our location to that zip code. After days of back and forth with the corporate office, they allowed us to move our office to that prime location in downtown Orlando, and we were able to work out a deal.

That was an example of integrity. When you do business with integrity, sometimes you pay it forward, and you don't realize what it's going to mean a year or two later. This gentleman could have easily told us that we would have to pay the full fee to the franchisor, split the fee with him, or refuse to give up the location at all. Instead, he based his business decision on our business

model, and integrity was important to him because he saw that it was important to us.

Remember, integrity is doing the right things when you have nothing to gain and when no one is watching.

Coincidentally, five years after we moved into our downtown Orlando location, we learned that the same franchisee was selling his business, and we were looking to buy. Because of our mutual respect and goodwill, it allowed us to have a win-win negotiation for the purchase of that office. We now own that office, the same business that we mentored seven years prior. This is truly an example of how integrity fosters an environment of future opportunities and goodwill.

HEDGEHOG HINTS:

❶ Identify what thoughts or actions the word **INTEGRITY** evokes.

❷ Analyze how have you created an environment of good will within your organization or with your colleagues.

Chapter 10:

Accountability

"Each day you are leading by example. Whether you realize it or not or whether it's positive or negative, you are influencing those around you."

~Rob Liano

Similar to integrity, accountability is a word that sometimes is misunderstood. But accountability means so much to us in our business that I count it an honor to share it from our point of view.

In 2012, as we were looking to launch our second office in South Florida, both Cassandra and I were working around the clock to manage the Orlando office and planning for the new office in South Florida. Now, I was driving back and forth to South Florida twice per week (about 1,000 miles on the car every two weeks). What I did not realize was that I was putting mileage on my body as well. A month before we opened the office, Cassandra reminded me that I had not been to the doctor in over a year. That was five years ago, and I was 37 years old. I weighed in at about 180 pounds. Aside from the occasional feeling of being tired from the stress and workload, I never had any other health issues. Physically, I looked and felt fine. However, when I visited the doctor and had some tests done, I learned that I had high cholesterol. I was shocked. How could I, a healthy man who is not overweight and who looks and feels fine, have this type of result?

What Are Your Vital Signs?

The doctor explained to me that a person's vital signs are not a measure of a single test but a combination of many tests that result in an overall bill of health. Additionally, he said that certain metrics not only can affect other metrics, but many of them impact each other. I was surprised to hear the results about my health and high cholesterol. It was then that I realized that business works in the same way, where a combination of all the little things can have a large impact on the overall.

Shortly after we opened the office in South Florida, Cassandra assumed the responsibility to lead the Orlando office. I was in South Florida for six months prior to my family moving there. This leadership role was foreign to Cassandra because she had not led many teams before. She worked hard and prepared to step into that role. I was confident in her because she's a natural leader. We learned a lot during that transition in leadership. For the first two to three years in business we understood that we needed to be successful, but we never sat down and identified all of the key metrics that we needed to effectively manage and hold our team and ourselves accountable. I have to admit, the first couple of years we did not have the proper tools in place. Although we were doing fine by opening a second office, and we were the number one performing office in the country for the All County franchise system, we were not efficiently controlling the business in terms of its overall health.

This became very apparent in our weekly and monthly meetings. During one meeting, we recognized a young man for his business performance. But not everyone was applauding. They clearly knew something that we didn't. When I investigated further, I realized why. While the young man was a great salesperson, he had not been a good property manager when it came to retaining his clients. And his customer skills were also lacking because he would lose clients as fast as he was gaining them. In other words, the overall health of his business was not positive, and the team knew it, but they didn't know how to articulate that to us. I liken a business' vital signs to a student's GPA. Everyone understands that doing well in one subject doesn't mean you're a good student. It's your overall GPA that gives a better summary of the overall performance.

Therefore, we needed a method to look at the **overall health** of our business. So, Cassandra and I decided to do something about it; we made it our personal project to solve this. The issue was to stop looking at our business in silos and instead start taking a holistic approach. So, during our long drives back and forth to South Florida, we discussed what we could do to address this issue. It dawned on me that I needed to identify the key performance indicators for my business and measure them, instead of simply looking at each of them in isolation.

While I was working for Sprint in my early 20s, I remember sitting in the monthly vital signs meetings that the leadership team would have. They called them *vital signs meeting*s because the lead team had figured out all of the key performance indicators necessary to measure the health of that business. This was critical because I learned how these types of meetings helped the entire team in terms of accountability. My boss would talk about what the vital signs say about the health of our business. These meetings were always my favorite because I had the opportunity to see firsthand how each key performance metric impacted the business and how they worked together.

So, Cassandra and I set out to work hard to recreate the vital signs system of accountability in our business. After two months of brainstorming and consulting the team, we came up with nine key performance indicators that we would look at, not just on a monthly basis, but on a daily basis for our business to see how we were performing.

1. Net new contracts
2. Properties leased
3. Lease renewals
4. Delinquency percentage
5. Maintenance management
6. Days on the market (DOM)
7. Marketing activities
8. Bills management
9. Manager on Duty
10. Escalations/reputation management

The levers you can pull will positively affect the key performance indicators of your business. While working on implementing these indicators into our company, we learned a lot about our business and how to control the result. But, most importantly, we learned how to corral the team around the idea of self-accountability. Accountability is knowing what you're responsible for and knowing how to control the outcome.

Now, this is not just true for a property management business; this is true for any company. Having an accountability tool that allows you to manage or look at your key performance indicators certainly affects accountability. As leaders, we must design a system to hold our team accountable. If done right, the system will do much of the work. What I mean by that is, we did not know by identifying the key performance indicators that they were going to work so closely together and impact each other. We train everyone on how to maximize their performance on each of these individual key performance indicators and give them specifics on what to do. We dug even deeper by ensuring that everyone, not just the property managers but also the staff, was part of managing the overall vital signs of each office. In order to be successful, we gain buy-in from everyone. While it did not happen overnight, from an accountability perspective, every metric that we measured was improved upon.

Accountability Measures

Through this, I think we revolutionized accountability in our office. We believe that every business leader can do this if they take the time to follow the process. So, what exactly is the process? I believe that putting together an accountability measure requires strong leadership. First, every leader needs to **identify**

what success looks like to them. A leader must understand and have a vision for success. If you remember, in an earlier chapter I mentioned that in our office there is a chart that is permanently affixed to our wall. This chart shows what success looks like. It highlights a management team's vision of success.

Before we launched our business, we considered what it would take to be successful. One of our thoughts was to make sure that we had raving fans as owners. In order to boost our business and solidify our company, we needed owners that raved about our performance and about the level of service that we delivered to them. We wanted to ensure that we focused on what makes our clients raving fans, because what is most important to them should be important to us.

Next, you must **have a method to identify the key performance indicators** as they relate to the overall measure of success for your company. Key performance indicators will help to drive your vision home with your employees/team members. Then, your **team members in your office should also be on board** for your vision for success. You can't do it all alone, and there is a reason they are a part of your team; they must also have buy-in. Next, you must **roll out your new strategy**, but make sure that you monitor progress regularly. In the beginning, we measured progress monthly, and that was good. But we quickly realized that once you set up a **system of tracking your monthly success-measuring results,** you are then able to have something tangible—most importantly measurable—to work from. You can see what strategies or practices didn't work last month that may be effective in a new month, which is what we did for a few months after we launched the vital signs.

It wasn't the perfect system, but it was better than nothing. However, we quickly realized that when we were looking at the

results two weeks after the month ended, and we couldn't impact the results for that previous month. Instead, we realized we needed to focus more on accountability and decided to identify two or three of those vital signs and performance indicators and drill down on them on a weekly basis while we could still impact the game. In other words, if you're looking at football or basketball as an analogy, you don't try to evaluate and critique what went wrong in a lost game from the coach's perspective. Rather, the better option is to evaluate it on a play-by-play or quarter-by-quarter perspective, so you can change the overall trajectory of your results by the end of the month.

When we began doing that, we saw accountability skyrocket. We realized that our people were capable of managing to these indicators, but we as leaders needed to step up and give them the key indicators to measure. People will do what you measure. In other words, if you fail to inspect what you expect, then critical tasks may not get done. Often, this happens because employees believe that if it were important, it would be tracked and measured. As a result of this accountability, there's a sense of competition among the team. Every week leading to the end of the month, everyone on the team is looking at their individual performance, and there's a sense of competition that challenges each of them to do more and perform better.

So, the last process to an accountability vital signs plan is to ensure that the **team can present and speak to their result**. Now, that may seem like something simple. Here's what it's done for us. In the beginning, we were looking at the result, but we quickly realized that in order to hold the people accountable, they needed to come to the meeting and tell us about their performance. You may be wondering why this is effective. Well, this process produces many things. First, it ensures that team members know their business. If you call my Orlando office, or any other office, my property managers know their result for each of these performance indicators. They are not in the dark about the important numbers and how those numbers indicate the company's success results. Not only that, but if a member of a team is presenting their business results between five and seven minutes a month, there's a sense of competition with other team members to excel and do better next time.

Lastly, we stack rank our people, which means that we rank them from top performer to lowest performer in every category. For example, in the area of delinquency, which is basically outstanding rent over gross potential rent, we rank the team from the person with the lowest delinquency to the person with the highest delinquency. No one wants to be at the bottom of the ranking, but we also recognize those who are at the very top of the ranking. As a leader, it is important to identify the top two or three people and find out why they are ranking so high. We evaluate them and determine what they are doing differently than the people at the bottom.

There is an amazing book that was written 20 years ago by Jack Welch, the former chairman and CEO of General Electric, one of America's largest companies. This company has been around for over 100 years. The name of his book was *Jack: Straight from the Gut*. He mentions in his book that by ranking your people in terms of their performance, you automatically create a system of accountability because no one wants to be at the bottom. This was a way to ensure that everyone knew where they stood in their respective roles.

This system of accountability also guaranteed that if for some reason you have to part ways with someone on your team who was consistently ranking at the bottom, there would be no fight because they would have already understood their position or ranking in the company. From a positive perspective, this system of accountability provided the top-ranking employees acknowledgment and a reward for their hard work. Accountability on all fronts helps to improve the overall health of any business.

HEDGEHOG HINTS:

❶ Identify your key performance indicators (or KPIs).

❷ Inspect what you expect.

❸ Broadcast your team's results.

Chapter 11:

Communication

> "Communication—the human connection—is the key to personal and career success."
>
> ~Paul J. Meyer

I'm sure you're not too old to remember the telephone game that we all used to play as children, the one where one person starts off by whispering a "secret message" to the first player in a row of players. Then, that first player relays that same message to the next player, who then passes the message to the next person and so on. The game continues this way until the last person gets the message and has to share the secret out loud with the very first player who started the game. Usually, that message is not the same one as the original, not even close. One thing this game teaches is the importance of communication—effective communication. If a message is not communicated accurately, it can negatively impact the connection you form between you and others in business. However, you must first be clear on what effective communication is.

Communication is imparting or exchanging information or news, the successful conveying or sharing of ideas and feelings. It creates a connection between people or places; in particular, it means communication involves sending or receiving information through a telephone or computer or sending an email. Communication can be verbal, nonverbal, or written. With so many ways to communicate, how is it that we often miss the mark? In relationships and in business, issues can primarily be pinned on one culprit: miscommunication.

Communicating as a Value

Communication is the key component all leaders must have in order to be a leader people want to follow. I look at communication as a value in an equation that will lead to success. If you look at the previous chapters and combine them with communication, you'll find favorable results in your business. For example, if I went back to the proactive chapter and added communication to it, we would create the ability for all parties involved in a business to be on the same page and avoid any miscommunication. When we were launching a new aspect of our business and changing our business model, instead of just launching the business model and expecting everyone to fall in line, we took a proactive approach to our communication. We met with everyone on our team and explained to them what the new business model would be and how it would impact them. We gave them the opportunity to voice any concerns or objections they had so that we could address it then. Realistically, you may not be able to communicate with every employee each time you are implementing a change. However, when we skipped the communication component, the business felt the effects.

After we met with the team members individually, we would go ahead and roll out the new plan for our business in our team meeting. Being proactive in our communication allowed us to let the new business model idea settle in, as opposed to throwing people off guard and immediately thrusting our business model on them. It also prevented anarchy, if you will, because if your team questions what you are doing, then it creates a negative atmosphere in the office. Proactive plus communication allows everyone to feel comfortable, and it avoids any miscommunications.

When you **communicate your goals** to your team, it creates a target plan for everyone to follow. An example of this was the system of vital signs we created for evaluating our company's performance. Our goals communicated what was important in our business, the aspects of our business that really drive what we consider to be success. And because we communicated those goals and made it clear what we expected on a weekly, monthly, and quarterly basis, then it was no longer a moving target but a set target. Those goals that we communicated allowed the team to know what was expected of them and gave us the ability to monitor their progress and hold them accountable when necessary.

Prioritizing communication results in a more effective and efficient operation. The mistake that many of us make is that we get bogged down with the day-to-day duties, which most of us could delegate. So, if we communicate to the team members what we will delegate and exactly what we need in order to be successful, it will eliminate the need for micromanagement. You must trust the person that you are delegating to and then trust how you are communicating your needs to them. And after you've delegated a task, you must continue the communication by following up to make sure that it was done well. This frees you up from having to deal with the daily minutiae of business ownership and being in leadership so that you can focus on the high-level aspects of your business.

Win-win plus communication equals the possibilities for satisfactory outcomes. Sometimes it's not what you say, but it's how you say it. And you must do a great job of communicating what you want and why. You must make sure you communicate that you understand what the other side wants in order to try to make it work. When I was younger, my mother would wake up my brothers and me on a Saturday morning with her frustrations on the condition of the home. Needless to say, it wasn't a very great way to wake up in the morning, but in my mother's defense, she worked a demanding job, and the moment she got home from one of her late shifts, the last thing she wanted to see was a mess. She yelled at us to hurry us into action and created an urgency to get the house in order. We would get it done if we wanted to live or survive that day.

In contrast, my dad would come home and try to calm her frustrations by telling her to rest. Then, he would take over. My dad would appeal to our intellect. He knew there would be something we wanted to do during the weekends, like watch a movie or attend an event. He would simply say, "Let's get it done guys if you want to participate in any extracurricular activities." Now, they both had the same message but used a different approach. In retrospect, my mom motivated us into action to get the job done. The way she communicated caused us to be defensive and shut down. My dad, on the other hand, just wanted my mom to be happy and for us to get the job done. He knew that we would be self-motivated to get the job done if we knew what the payoff would be.

In business, I'm sure you've heard of many occasions where an individual had the credentials and the qualifications but lacked the ability to effectively run a department, lead a team, launch a project, close a deal, or maybe even resolve an issue. Conversely, I'm sure you've also heard of the complete opposite, when someone maybe was not so qualified and did not have all the credentials, but they were an effective communicator and excelled in all the same areas. Think about how you show up in the room and how people receive you based on how well you communicate.

Ralph Waldo Emerson once said, "Who you are speaks so loudly I can't hear what you're saying." I had to read that twice because the words were so impactful. When you present your ideas, seek the win-win for both sides and make sure that you communicate in a way that everyone receives the message.

Listening plus communication equals the allowance for you to know your audience. Listening and communicating go hand in hand. You can't effectively communicate unless you have a balance on both sides. When you take the time to listen before you speak, you become more effective in your communication because you understand the other person's point of view. Sometimes, just by acknowledging a person and communicating back what you understand facilitates the ability for your message to be received. You must communicate differently depending on who is receiving the message. That is why it's so important to get to know your team. Listen to your team. Everyone is different, and based on the relationship you have with them, it will determine the way the message is received.

When we moved into our new office, I had the option of sitting in the corner office, one closest to the back and away from the noise in the front of the building. I decided to take the office right in the middle, across from the team. I got to hear daily conversations with clients, tenants, vendors, and among team members. It gave me the opportunity to step in whenever they needed my guidance and to hear about their wins and losses. We got to celebrate with them or give encouragement when they did have issues or if there was a failure.

I was also able to offer on-the-spot coaching to avoid future problems. The best part was when we had personal, humorous, vulnerable, inspiring, and real conversations with each other. If you think about it, people spend the majority of their time at work with people that eventually become like their family. Moreover, during stressful times at work, the people that you work with can sometimes even alleviate some of that stress. A trust and a bond will form between you and your team members. I chose to listen to them and communicate well with them so that I understood them. This helped me to create a relationship with them—working shoulder to shoulder with the people that worked with me. And when I communicated, even when it was a tough conversation, there was a willingness from them to receive the feedback.

Now, let's take a look at **synergy plus communication**. Synergy is the ability to identify areas of weakness or lack of resources in your business and create partnerships to mitigate those areas. Consider this: compromise versus collaboration. Which one sounds better to you? Compromise can sound negative; it gives the impression that one would have to give something up for the better good. Collaboration, on the other hand, says, "I can contribute something for the greater good." Everyone has something to contribute if you create an environment that fosters inclusion and collaboration. Then you will have a team willing to partner to drive results—where one person is weak in a concept, another may be strong. We are much greater when we combine our efforts. When we share our weaknesses, others feel unafraid to do the same. You also create an environment of authenticity. Now, the real work can begin, and a plan can be formulated to tap the individuals to step in and partner with one another to make it work.

Growth plus communication equals a clear path to increasing the team's overall competency. Road maps are great, but if you have no idea where you're going, how will they help you? By creating a growth map for your team and communicating the path that you want everyone to take, the outcome will be that everyone is working on growing. As a result, the organization can grow by increasing the overall competency of each team member.

Communication is a big part of our core values. We incorporate activities that will increase our team member's ability to sharpen their communication skills. We would advise, for example, in our growth plan, that individuals on our team join their local Toastmasters chapter. Toastmasters—as I mentioned in a previous chapter—is a nonprofit organization that allows individuals to sharpen their communication skills. At the weekly meetings, people are assigned different areas to focus on for every short speech to help them hone in on a particular area of effective communication.

We also advise certain individuals on our team to practice the art of networking. By constantly putting yourself in a position to communicate your ideas, your thoughts, your business, your brand, and what you represent to someone else, you become more skilled in a very short time. It is a worthwhile opportunity.

The other thing we ask our people to do is to join organizations and get on the leadership team. This gives them opportunities to publicly present or communicate to an organization and trust that their effective communication will accomplish certain goals. We believe that these requirements of our team members help to drive the overall growth and the competency of our entire team.

Team Building

Building trust is a huge foundation of communication. Generally, if someone does not trust you or your brand/company they are not willing to listen well to what you have to say. Therefore, the way you communicate will not be effective in convincing them. So, there has to be some level of trust in communication. John Maxwell says, "People ultimately want to KNOW the following things: that they can trust you, that you care, and that you can help them."

Here is our advice on ways you can build trust in communication with your team members and potential clients:

❶ Have one-on-one conversations with your team members, but not just to communicate about a problem. When we had a new team member, and we opened our office in South Florida, it was difficult to get to know everyone on our team. One day Socrate said to me, "Sometimes, you have to call just to say, 'Hi. How are you doing?'" or "What's going on in your day today?" What you want to do is make it intentional that you're not only communicating with someone when there is a problem or when you're going to coach them, but you'll communicate with them just because. You don't want them to expect that every time they interact with you, it will be predictable or a reprimand.

You are then able to break down the walls and get to know your team members on an individual basis. And they know that you care about them when you reference things about their lives, like remembering one of their family members or that one of their children made the honor roll at school. And if they are struggling in a certain area, they know that you can help them because you're not coming from a place of criticism or regularly communicating only when there is a problem.

❷ Another thing that I learned is to use the *Sandwich Method* when communicating. The Sandwich Method is used when you have to coach someone on something that they're not doing so well. You start off by giving them kudos or compliments on what they are doing well in their business or daily tasks. And then you address the problem by speaking to the issue, while also presenting solutions to resolve it. Follow up by letting the person know how much you appreciate their contribution to the organization or how they add value.

❸ Use team-builder activities. Team builders allow an opportunity for the hierarchical walls to come down, and you give people a chance just to get to know each other on the same level, on the same playing field. This is neutral ground, if you will. And that's a way that you can build trust with your team so that when it comes time for you to communicate both the good and the not so good, those barriers have been lifted.

❹ Timing is everything. When it comes to communication, you want to make sure it's not only *what* you communicate, but it's *when* you communicate. I mentioned it before, but when you are launching a project or you are rolling out a new program in your organization, you want to make sure that you have a communication plan. I can't tell you how many times I've worked in an organization or I've been a part of a team, and something is being implemented or changed and I'm the last to hear about it. Therefore, it's critical that you use the right timing to launch anything. Communicate at the right time to all parties involved, and make sure that you answer all questions. Clarity is the top priority so that there's no confusion or miscommunication.

HEDGEHOG HINTS:

❶ Communicate early and often.

❷ Be intentional.

❸ Remember, "Everyone communicates but few connect." – John Maxwell

Chapter 12:

Teamwork

> "The strength of the team is each individual member. The strength of each member is the team."
>
> ~Phil Jackson, retired basketball coach and former player

What is teamwork? Why is teamwork effective? How do you build it? These are questions that you must ask yourself if you are to confidently and effectively build a business and create teamwork among yourself and your employees.

Principle-Based Decision Making

I want to start us off by talking about an approach called the **principle-based decision-making process**. This approach entails that we should base our decisions on values and principles rather than emotions. Principle-based decision making is founded on the use of ethical values and principles that guide our decisions. This approach, as well as other rule-based tactics, relies on the set of time-tested principles, such as honesty, respect, equality, fairness, and courage to guide our decisions.

From a leadership perspective, basing decisions on how you view your valued teamwork is critical. Additionally, leaders can foster that value throughout their organizations, regardless of the company's size or the team size. I come from a large family—I have nine brothers. My brothers and I always played sports, and most of them were team sports, so the concept of team was formed in me at a very early age in my household. There's so much to learn from sports as it relates to teamwork. In fact, my of my fondest memories growing up were either about watching my favorite sports teams play or participating in sports with my brothers and friends.

I remember playing Little League soccer on the same team with my brothers. One of my closest brothers in age was Jouvens, a younger brother. During practice, we would always go at each other and compete as if we're playing for a trophy. Yet, the next day we would travel to compete with another team, and we were united; we worked together because we were part of a team. I remember vividly when we traveled across town to play against a competitor in Pompano Beach. Often, we were coming from a lower economic part of town and traveling to a more affluent part of town.

We were always a little nervous before the games because we knew what to expect: We were going to play a team that was probably more organized and more equipped than we were. They had all the goods that we didn't, and they were always bigger and stronger than we were. I remember walking onto the field and looking at our competitors; they looked like they were a college team. They had the shorts, matching shirts, matching socks, matching shoes, and overalls. We could never afford any of these things. On that day, we nervously looked at each other, knowing we were outmatched in terms of preparation. But, surprisingly (maybe not so surprisingly), we passed the ball. We did not argue with each other on the field like we had done during practice all week. We just played together, and we played to win.

The point is that we learned how to support each other and work together as a team toward a common goal, regardless of how hard we practiced against one another throughout the week. We learned this from great coaches who fostered the environment of teamwork, and we learned how that teamwork could help us thrive.

From a business perspective, knowing how to work in teams and ensure optimal team performance is key for anyone. As leaders, we are like coaches. Our job is to create teams, direct teams, and inspire teams to achieve our business goals. It's fascinating how much more we can accomplish with teamwork. This is also true in relationships. Cassandra and I met in 2000 and began dating in 2001. We both had certain goals and aspirations. I had already completed my bachelor's degree, and Cassandra was in her senior year at UCF. We worked for different companies. I was already in the workforce and she was working a part-time job as a student, but we were in different industries. When we started dating seriously, I can remember sitting down with Cassandra and mapping out our vision and goals as a couple. While this seemed a little strange for a couple to do—even Cassandra found it strange—these exercises ultimately helped us get on the same page and work together as our own small team. After becoming life partners, we eventually decided to become business owners, and we've accomplished quite a bit in 18 years together, with the last eight years as business partners.

Understanding the Stages of Team Development

There are business principles and habits that leaders should know in order to maximize team performance. More specifically, there are a set of developmental life cycles, or stages, that I want to pinpoint. These stages of team development are **forming, storming, norming, performing, and adjourning**. These stages of team development are used in building teams: project teams or long-term teams. Knowing these stages is critical. At any given time, a leader may be working with different groups that are in different stages of this cycle. The goal of knowing each stage of the cycle is to understand how to maximize performance at each of the stages in order to get the most out of and from each individual on your team. The stages of team development are often referenced in project management professional books. This theory has been written about for decades and illustrate every team going through cycles from inception through adjourning. The key concept is for the leader to recognize the stages and maximize team performance at each stage.

Forming — This is the stage where people come together. This may be where new people are joining an existing group in your company and you, the leader, begin assigning individuals project. Usually at this stage, members feel uncertain and confused about the team goal, the structure and leadership, and who does what. The team members may attempt to understand and define their roles and responsibilities. Therefore, in this stage, the key for leaders is to clearly define boundaries and structure to minimize any misunderstanding and designate each person's responsibilities. A leader can coordinate simple things like ice breakers to allow the team to get to know each other, have meetings to define responsibilities, organize the reporting and communications structure, or determine the days and times when team members will meet.

Storming — At this stage team members sometimes will test their position and challenge other team members. At times, the team members may clash and confront each other regarding the goals, their tasks, and their responsibilities. Some may even divide into opposing groups to support their cause. This is something I've seen quite a lot in my company. We have three locations, as you know, and every time we separate the group into smaller teams to accomplish a goal, we often see that the groups, even the smaller teams, subdivide themselves into opposing groups to support their causes.

Some may even compete for a desired role and responsibility. Team members may begin to refine the pattern of interaction, and some may choose to withdraw and not participate. Now, you may assume that this is just immature behavior and they just need to get over it; however, you must remember that you are dealing with real people, not scenarios or hypotheticals. Therefore, there is a level of respect or understanding that you must show for their feelings without being dismissive. The leader's role in this stage is to allow members to share their thoughts in a positive setting. Otherwise, storming can slow down the progress. While some leaders don't like to deal with this stage, sometimes storming is necessary to get to the norming and performing stages that follow. It is important to go through all the stages to be successful. If the storming stage does not happen at the beginning of your team formation, you can bet it may happen at a more crucial stage and perhaps at the wrong time, so it is critical that you take care of it immediately as it happens.

Norming — During this stage, team members begin to settle into their roles and responsibilities—cooperating and collaborating with each other. The teams begin to form their identity and they begin to appreciate each other and their differences. Moreover, this is the stage when the team members begin to recognize and appreciate one another's strengths and differences—not just their similarities.

Team members begin exchanging ideas more freely as they begin to open up to each other. You may also observe team members working toward a goal, and they interact more according to what has been accepted by the team because their leader has laid the groundwork and expectations for them to follow from the beginning.

While as leaders we may set the tone, during the norming stages, the team eventually needs to take on its own identity. In the norming stage, they will begin to manage themselves according to what's acceptable for the team, which leads to the next stage: performing.

Performing — This is most leaders' favorite stage. As the team is using "performing" consistently, they usually maintain their level of effectiveness by focusing and accomplishing results as it relates to the goals. By this stage, everyone knows his or her responsibilities. They trust each other to do their part and celebrate each other's individual contributions.

I have observed more accountability when the teams addressed each other's shortcomings without leadership having to intervene, resulting in well-received feedback. Surprisingly, the leaders can enhance this stage by allowing the team to be self-managed, while they offer little guidance so as not to disrupt the momentum and flow.

We do this on a regular basis at our offices, particularly with our more seasoned team at our Orlando office. We often assign projects to them and divide them into subgroups. However, since they are four hours away, we allow them to be self-managed. And when we do show up to that office via conferencing or in person, we step away and allow them to continue on with the performing stage because we don't want to disrupt the momentum they've formed. Additionally, a leader works to maximize this stage and get the best out of each individual and the team's performance overall by continuing to let the team be self-managed. In fact, it pleases us to see them working this way because we are then confident that the project will get done and get done well.

Adjourning — This is a stage where members begin leaving the group. If it's a project team, they will begin leaving because the project has ended (and hopefully it has ended successfully). If the team has been successful, the members are usually positive about the team's accomplishments and their individual contributions. However, there are instances, depending on why the adjourning is happening, team members may feel a sense of loss instead of accomplishment. The leader can help by having a final meeting celebrating the team's successes and acknowledging each person's role on the team.

Too often, this stage is forgotten. After we perform, we accomplish our goal. Yet, sometimes leaders don't do anything to ensure that recognitions are handed out to team members or even to help and organize the next project. If someone has devoted their time and energy to a team project, it is important to close the chapter out well because people do have a sense of loss when a project or team ends abruptly without a final adjourning phase.

Teamwork

Having managed several teams and currently leading four different groups in three different locations, I recognize that each of my teams, whether it be South Florida, Orlando, or Jacksonville is at a different stage of their development. My Orlando team, for example, has been in business for close to eight years, so they're almost always in the performing stage. However, when you introduce new members to the group, you revert to a previous stage in the team development.

For this reason, I recommend that leaders take a situational management approach when dealing with teams. In other words, deal with each team and each person on said team differently based on the situation and on the individual. This, of course, will require you as a leader to get to know your team members personally. The plus is that knowing the predictable stages of team development is critical to maximizing performance at each stage.

Maximizing Teamwork

I'd like to share with you some quick tips to maximizing teamwork:

1. Know and understand the stages of team development.

2. Know what to do in each stage — I can remember talking to Cassandra a few years ago when she was managing a team. They were clearly in the forming stage, approaching the storming stage. She began voicing her concerns to me saying, "What's happening? This is not the way I thought it was going to be." I calmly told her the clashing and confrontation that was starting to occur among team members who were pushing some boundaries was normal. If it didn't happen at that stage, it was eventually going to happen at the worst time. I

just told her to let it happen and that her job was to ensure that whatever disagreement or jockeying she was seeing, she should just continue to lead and guide them well through it, making sure that it didn't get out of control. So, you don't just need to know what to do, but you must be prepared to handle the issues that may come up.

3. Accept the unexpected — No matter how much you know the stages of team development, it's also important to keep in mind that there will be the unexpected. By that I mean you may end one stage and think you are done with it and ready to move on to the next stage. However, you may end up watching your team revert and go back to the beginning phase again. This means that the stage prior to that was not completed successfully, so you have no choice but to lead and guide your team back to the previous stage and decipher what went wrong.

   We see this all the time. I'll use a sports analogy again as an example. You may have a team that is performing quite well, but for some reason, they begin to lose their momentum and within the next weeks or months, they end up on a downward spiral. What happened was they ended up back at the storming stage again. The goal for leaders when something like that happens is to manage the storming stage and then minimize it. You must make sure it's addressed so that there are no hidden agendas happening in the storming stage that will rear their ugly heads again at the worst time. From a sports perspective, the last thing you want to see is division and confrontation among team members happening at the finals game or a critical championship game. That stage should've been dealt with early on during the team's stage of development, and handled properly to minimize it from happening.

4. Understand that the team may revert to previous stages — This is something that took me, and maybe some other leaders, by surprise. Just when you think you're done with the storming stage or the performing stage, you end up reverting back to the previous stage because things were left unresolved. Or maybe you added someone new to the team and it changed the team dynamic. It's important to note that any time you add a new person to the team, they may go through their own stages personally, and the team may also go through it in a smaller way after just adding a few people to the team.

The important thing is for the leaders to first be aware of the stages, but more importantly, they should know how to progress through each stage. Ultimately, the goal is to arrive at and maximize the performing stage and minimize any negative impacts during other stages.

SECTION 3:

The Capstone

Chapter 13:

Sacrifice

"Entrepreneurship is living a few years of your life like most people won't, so that you can spend the rest of your life like most people can't."

~ Anonymous

There is a tendency in our society toward a fascination with fame and fortune. You can ask young children what they want to be when they grow up, and famous is oftentimes the No. 1 answer. Some might want to liken their lives to and emulate a famous pop star, an athlete, an actor, or an actress. We admire people that are doing well, but we often don't take the time to understand what it took for them to get there. And what it took was **sacrifice**.

Sacrifice involves effort and hard work. Hard work is one element most people want to avoid. Why? Because it's not an endeavor you do once; it is continually done. And it also requires that you relinquish something as well—perhaps something of great value—in order to gain something of even greater value.

The moment a leader decides that they no longer have to make any sacrifices, then their business suffers and so do their people. Sacrifice means that even when things get tough, you refer back to your values and make the tough decisions that most people would rather run away from. Are you willing to make some sacrifices? Look at your circumstances. What would you be willing to give up to live your dream? What would that look like for you?

When Socrate and I decided to get into business, we had to make the tough decision to walk away from our lifestyle and our income and risk stepping into an unknown future. Socrate was a senior operations' manager at Sprint, making a six-figure salary; I was a manager for a large property management company. To anyone else, we would be crazy to walk away from financial stability like this. We also had two small children at the time, and we knew that the risk would be great, but we were willing to make the sacrifice because we envisioned more for our lives and theirs. Little did we know the sacrifices would be great. We had to reduce costs to pay the bills and to finance our new business venture. We couldn't even pay ourselves in the first two years. We had to dip into our savings and sacrifice just to pay our employees.

> **Instant gratification is the death of progress.**

On the outside, our business was doing well. We were growing, and we were making progress. However, we were not at the point where we could take home a paycheck. Our finances began to suffer, and we had to tighten the belt even further, which propelled me to start watching extreme couponing on television to get cost-saving tips. Every Sunday, I would be the first at the grocery store to

get my three Sunday papers. I had my scissors and binder ready to organize my coupons and prepare my grocery list to maximize my savings. This became my weekly ritual for several years. I had to scale back on dinners and entertainment, and I also discovered Netflix. I learned to put my vanity aside and mastered my own beauty care. Behind us, we were losing all the things we worked hard for as a family. But ahead of us, was a growing, bright future. The difficulty was reminding ourselves of that bright future. The truth is that no one would have been mad or disappointed in us if we stopped everything at that point and went right back to the lifestyle we were living before. But we had sacrificed too much to quit.

At this point, we were experiencing the real meaning of sacrifice—not focusing on what you can gain from today, but what you can build for tomorrow. And we were certainly building our team and gaining momentum. We were even looking into an opportunity to expand our offices in another Florida market. Yet, this was when we reached a crossroads: We could pursue that opportunity to tap into the South Florida market or just focus on building our current business. This way, we could perhaps turn our finances around and save our home. Or we could take another leap of faith and sacrifice our security by pursuing another business market.

The sacrifices continued, and despite all our efforts, we did have to let our home go and even sell a few pieces of furniture for cash. We left behind our 4000-square-foot, five-bedroom home, in a gated community, with a pool and packed up and moved to South Florida, from Orlando to a non-gated, 1200-square-foot condo in a not-so-great area.

Sacrifices That Lead to Success

We were not where we wanted to be, but our family was together, and we had everything we needed. Would you be willing to make those sacrifices to build your team or your dream? And how much would be too much? Now, fast-forward to our present lives, and I can gladly tell you that we made the right decision. We were able to grow exponentially in both markets because we decided to take the risk and make that move to South Florida.

Consequently, we landed a contract with the fourth largest institutional investor in the country. Our Orlando office has been the top franchise office in the country for five consecutive years, and we're pushing to finish at the top for this year. We have also been able to launch a third office in Jacksonville, and a fourth in Lake Mary. We are rapidly growing and setting our sights on other markets.

So, we hope our story serves as an example of how you can't always judge a book by its cover, or rather, judge a person by their possessions/successes before knowing the story behind it. Consider what sacrifices it took for them to get there. You may be surprised to learn what sacrifices someone will make to achieve success.

When Socrate moved to South Florida to open our company's second office, I was left in Orlando to run that office by myself. I was the salesperson out in the field beating the streets and managing a portfolio. That was where I was comfortable. I was in my element, and I could do it with my eyes closed. However, now I had to manage a business, plus everyone in it, which is not what I wanted to do. I would often get lost in what I did best and procrastinated or avoided the things I needed to get done or didn't like doing. As a result, things would slip through the cracks. I remember on one occasion, I missed the deadline to submit payroll, and our staff did not get paid on time. I was mortified. This lit a fire under me and motivated me to change what I was doing. I made the painstaking decision to give up my portfolio to my assistant Yarmmys Vargas. It was difficult because I had built the portfolio myself; I knew every owner and every property by heart. But, I knew this was a business sacrifice I needed to make or else I would continue to watch my role in the company wither.

In the beginning, I was unwilling to relinquish the control of my portfolio to Yarmmys, and I certainly didn't want to micromanage her. Yet, I couldn't resist double checking her work until I felt confident that she had it under control. I soon realized that relinquishing control to her was the best decision I ever made. It allowed me to focus solely on the success of our business, enabling me to identify the issues that were occurring on a consistent basis.

Socrate and I were able to create the vital signs to monitor our progress regularly. The intangible effect was that Yarmmys emerged as a leader. She became my right hand. She has since been promoted to operations manager of our office in Orlando. Much credit goes to her because without her we probably wouldn't have been able to let go of control in Orlando and expand into South Florida. She allowed us to trust that our business was being taken care of.

To continue to be successful, leaders must make sacrifices because growth stops when the price gets too high. In other words, growth stops when you are unwilling or unable to make any more sacrifices. You must be willing to let go or adjust your role in your business or organization for growth to take place. Ask yourself, what is your highest and best use? As leaders, we tend to have this idea that no one can get it done the way we can do it. This may be true. However, you cannot do it all. Sometimes we

Sacrifice

spend too much time with our head down getting things done, neglecting to look up and acknowledge what's happening in our business. Essentially, you're not actually working on the business because you're too busy *working in the business.*

Socrate and I often travel across the country to work with business owners and leaders. And in doing so, we find that sometimes there is a tendency for them to spend entirely too much time on tasks that should be delegated to their team members. When we conduct a business analysis, we can attribute the inconsistencies, failures, inefficiencies, or department breakdowns to a lack of attention. Essentially, there is no one paying attention to the production of the operation or strategizing to mitigate the threats and the weaknesses.

Another great benefit to sacrificing control and allowing our team members to run point while we focused on the successful growth of our business was that we realized if we set the right checks and balances in place, we didn't have to be in the office for it to run successfully. When Socrate would travel back and forth on the weekends to spend time with us after being gone all week—and then do it all over again when he would head back on Monday—it was very taxing on him physically, mentally, and emotionally to be away from his family. Eventually, I was able to join Socrate a few months later in South Florida with our children. We both knew that making that sacrifice for our family was difficult, but also necessary. Once we were reunited, we were both able to focus on building the South Florida office.

So just to recap, know that sacrifice is not a one-time payment. It's ongoing. Growth stops when the price gets too high. When the sacrifice required is no longer one that you are willing to make, you have to know what your highest and best use is, and then delegate the rest. When you delegate, you allow other people on your team to take on the roles that may not be best suited for you. Pride should never have a seat at a leader's table. You must put it aside for the sake of the team and take responsibility when things are not going right with either an individual or the team. When you want to apply the principle of sacrifice in your business, ask the following questions: Where do I want to be? What am I willing to give up? And who am I going to take with me?

HEDGEHOG HINTS:

❶ Sacrifice is not a one-time payment.

❷ Ask yourself what sacrifice you are willing to make to reach your goals.

❸ Identify the biggest professional sacrifice you have made.

Chapter 14:

Legacy

"To whom much is given...much will be required."

~ Luke 12:48 (ESV)

This Bible verse above is one of my favorites. However, there are times when I think it can be misunderstood to read that only when much is given much is required. But, there's more to it. I believe that something should be required by everyone, regardless of how much he or she has been given. Wouldn't you agree? The late Maya Angelou once wrote, "When you get, give. When you learn, teach." I believe that is a universal principle that is designed to advance the human race. The sooner we come to this realization, the further we can make quantum leaps in society.

What has been left behind to someone from generations is what has been passed down to you, and only you can determine what you do with it. This is what translates into your legacy. No matter how large or small, all of us have some kind of legacy that we will leave for someone else to follow. Does one have to be given much to be able to leave a significant legacy? And what kind of legacy will you leave?

You may remember in an earlier chapter when I shared that I had the privilege to attend the late, great Stephen Covey's conference on *The 7 Habits of Highly Effective People*. And I've mentioned Covey quite a lot throughout the book. Before attending his conference as a 19-year-old student, I had not previously given much thought to the idea of beginning with the end in mind. It's not exactly common for a 19-year-old to be thinking about the end at that time in their lives. Nevertheless, a seed was planted in me to think about always beginning with the end in mind, and it was crystallized from that time after.

Leaving Your Mark

I've mentioned before that my parents are immigrants from Haiti. Cassandra's parents are as well. My mom only completed an elementary education; my dad had some high school education, but he didn't finish. Growing up in a household full of boys in the '80s was tough for me, especially when I think about how very little we had. We were poor. I didn't see it then, but I know now we were poor. During the summer after my fifth-grade year, I remember asking my mom if she could sign me up for the local boys and girls club, which was only $15 a month, believe it or not. At the time, there were three of us living with my parents. My mother said, "If I sign you up, I would have to sign up your brothers, and that would be $45 a month. I can't afford that amount because I need to pay the water bill." While my parents could not give us a lot of monetary items, they gave to us in other ways. They often asked us about whom we wanted to surround ourselves with. Later on, I understood that to mean the

Law of the Inner Circle. You see, my dad would always say, "If you show me the five people you spend the most amount of time with, I will show you where you're going to be in five years." As a result, Cassandra's and my inner circle was rather small, only a small group of friends. Most of my brothers are now married with children and are working hard to live out their dreams and create a legacy in their own professions. Carefully picking your inner circle will have a direct effect on your success and, thus, on your legacy. People come first.

Even with a very limited education my parents understood and taught all their children legacy principles. These principles are: **giving, the inner circle, people come first, and start at home.**

Often, when one thinks about legacy, the thought is immediately about the end. However, we wanted to focus on our now, on what we are doing now, because this is what would then lead to the legacy we wanted to create for our children.

The point is that the only way we can progress as a society is to teach and give. From a legacy perspective, if the only thing you can leave behind when it's all over is knowledge, then pass that on. The next generation may be able to take that knowledge and apply it in a way that you never did in order to multiply its success. The world is full of people who have started with very little, yet they have made enormous contributions to the world and left legacies that will forever be remembered.

As business leaders, we are lucky to have an amazing team of people who are willing to share and give freely to those who are coming behind them, sharing the lessons they have learned. We have systems and processes in place that facilitate the exchange of ideas. For example, one of the simple things we do at the office is we have our people share what they've learned after they've attended a conference or class. This ensures that there's a level of accountability in knowing that you must share a lesson you've learned. It also helps others who did not attend the class or the training pick up some important nuggets while building team cohesiveness.

During our monthly vital signs meeting, we have our property managers give an overview of their portfolios. Each one manages between 50 and 150 properties. During these meetings, they all share their best practices with the team. We find that a lot of teaching and learning takes place during this time because each person gets an opportunity to share. These monthly meetings have become my personal favorite for a lot of reasons. When I first moved to South Florida in 2012, I joined a group called BNI, which stands for Business Network International. BNI is the world's largest networking organization with chapters across the globe. BNI's philosophy is "givers gain." This philosophy basically means that while one should not give in order to gain, those of us who give willingly and freely know something others do not know. We know that giving is an intrinsic universal law. When done, you will receive much more in return. This will not necessarily happen by the same person you gave to, but you will gain, nonetheless. It is a proven principle.

During my time at BNI, my company and I gave over 3.5 million dollars in business to the members of the group. The interesting thing is, while I did not receive a ton of business from the members of the group, I received referrals and business from other sources. From a legacy perspective, you can create goodwill in your community that will produce long-term, intangible benefits long after you are gone.

Consequently, my business grew exponentially during that time, with most coming from referral sources that I had not given any business. From a legacy perspective, when you give, you can often change someone's path by your generosity. When you affect someone's future for the better by your actions, you're operating in the legacy space or mindset. Likewise, I recognized that I'm also living someone's legacy because of the sacrifice my parents made and the guidance of many mentors who have poured into my life—both professionally and personally.

Back in the '70s, when the banking industry was in turmoil, Dick Cooley was president and CEO of Wells Fargo. While meeting with the board of directors about his role, Mr. Cooley was asked about his vision and his plan for success. He responded, "I have a vision, but I don't have a plan yet." Surprisingly, the board asked him to elaborate. He then explained that he first needed to get the right people on the bus. Then, he would get the wrong people off the bus. And finally, he would get the right people on the right seat on the bus.

The idea behind this was that he wanted people to understand that before you can go far in life, you must first surround yourself with the right people. As business owners, one of the most important, if not the most important, roles we have is to have the right people on our team. Our experience as business owners of multiple offices for our company has allowed us to have a keen eye for finding, hiring, and keeping the right people for our team. John Maxwell wrote, "Leadership is not how far we advance ourselves but how far we advance others." With that thought in mind, you will create a culture of legacy. Below, are **four** points that address this:

First, if you want to manage committed people, you must **hire committed people**. Committed to what, you may ask. Essentially, they must be committed to what matters to you—to your legacy—while having a strong desire to create their own.

While this sounds very simple, it's actually easier said than done, for sure. The good news is it *is* possible.

Secondly, you must be **slow to hire and quick** to part ways. Often, we take an enormous amount of time to hire people. As a result, we regretfully may have passed on some good talent along the way. However, you must trust your process. Conversely, we try to part ways quickly with folks who don't belong in our team because they are not the right fit.

Next, **invest in people**. One of the best ways, you can grow your business to create a lasting legacy is to help your people grow. As we wrote in the growth chapter, this should be at the top of every leader's list. Remember, by increasing the overall competency of your team, you raise the level of professionalism, efficiency, and productivity of your business.

Finally, **add value to people**. When you add value to people, whether by teaching, coaching, or mentoring, you're building a bridge connecting your legacy and their legacy. In Chapter 2, I wrote about attending my first funeral at the age of 34. I guess I was lucky that I had not experienced many deaths of loved ones up to that point. Sadly, as I wrote this chapter, my dear friend whose mother's funeral I attended 10 years ago passed away last week. During his mother's funeral, I learned that your legacy lives in those and through those whom you've impacted. While I didn't know her well, I knew her son, Mr. Rufus Mosley. I then realized that he implemented a lot of what he learned from his mom in how he handled business. As a result, his mother's legacy impacted many people directly through her life and then his as an extension of her.

All of these characteristics are linked to creating a worthwhile legacy because they require you to ACT. To put it plainly, your actions will lead to your legacy. Oftentimes, it is whether you want it to or not. Where do you want your actions to lead?

☙

Unfortunately, in 2018, I had the sad experience of speaking at Mr. Rufus Mosley's funeral. I mourned with the family as I shared what he meant to me. The most touching speaker, though, was his amazingly vibrant young daughter, Amber, who spoke and vowed to carry on his legacy of hard work and perseverance. I have no doubt the legacy of her grandmother will live on through her and her siblings. When you add value to people, you are leaving a legacy like a wildfire that will continue long after it has been ignited. We are working hard to leave a legacy in our business with those whom we've been entrusted to lead, coach, and mentor.

Our Children

Start at home

An added blessing for Cassandra and me is having two of the most incredibly talented little people to parent. From the moment that Cassandra and I met, we knew we wanted kids. When we first got married, we had plenty of time to discuss how we wanted to raise our future children. Less than two years after Cassandra gave birth to our daughter Arylan, our son was born. Needless to say, we became very busy, very fast. Our lives are constantly busy managing business ownership and family life, and we wouldn't have it any other way. Through our children, most importantly, the evidence of our legacy will be revealed.

Therefore, we want to ensure that we pour into them the best of who we are, including the best of our time.

From a business perspective, I have found that leaders who had a balanced or well-rounded life tend to relate better to different situations in their business. For example, before I was married and had kids, I was not as sympathetic as I could've been to parents who were coming in late because they had to drop off their kids at school first or had to leave early for a school function. I have found that life experience is a great teacher for any leader. Starting at home also means that the leader must be authentic, and that undoubtedly begins with those closest to you. Most importantly, you must try to lead, or live out, the principles of integrity around your family first—those you will leave a legacy for.

As copreneurs, Cassandra and I have the awesome opportunity to work and live life together. And we can honestly say that we enjoy it because our spirits are connected; therefore our visions are aligned both personally and professionally. From a legacy perspective, we have written down our desires, and we continue to be amazed at what we have accomplished by doing so.

At the end of the day, that's why we're in business—to create a lasting legacy. Likewise, this is the same reason we don't take certain jobs or specific travel requests that come in because we have to keep in mind how every decision we make affects our family.

What I learned from my friend's recent funeral was that no matter how much money you have, no matter how many houses you have, it is the people you touch and the legacy you leave behind that matters most. At his funeral, no one talked about what car he drove or where he lived, but we talked about what he meant to his family and what he's leaving behind for the people that he touched.

A legacy leaves an indelible and unique mark on your life and the lives of those you leave behind. When you are intentional about leaving a legacy, you live your life and run your business in a different way than your counterparts—a way that creates a vision, has a purpose, provides value, and is full of hope.

This is why it is imperative to find your why. I hope that both Cassandra and I were able to articulate our *why* as business owners and as people effectively. We firmly believe that our actions now will lead to a legacy that's much bigger than what we could ever imagine.

This final chapter on legacy brings home our hearts in pursuing our purpose in business and building upon a lasting foundation.

Conclusion

Almost 20 years ago, I began journaling some of the major events and learning experiences that I went through while searching for my hedgehog. During this time, I did not know what I would end up doing exactly, but I knew that I wanted to find something that I was passionate about, something that I would be good/great at, and something that was profitable. It was not until I had those combined experiences that it became clear where my path was leading me, and that was to business ownership. Today, as we speak to people—whether it's one on one or a crowd of a thousand—one of the questions that I get asked the most is, "How do you find your hedgehog as a person or business?" My answer is often to start with passion and make sure that the necessary factors (skill and profit) are also present.

Another question that we often get asked is, "When should I leave my job and just go for it?" The answer is DON'T. At times, a person may misunderstand the title: *Find your hedgehog and stop working* to mean *Find your passion and quit your job and just go for it*. This is not the case. One can find their hedgehog working in a corporation, small business, profit, or nonprofit. The fact of the matter is 90 percent plus of people will not become business owners. Business ownership is not for everyone. There is nothing wrong with that. For example, we have many highly successful friends who are not business owners, and many of them are in their element; they are happy in their industry and their careers.

When you are in your wheelhouse, you will know. You will know because work stops being work. From a business owner's or business leader's perspective, you may have people working with you, and as a leader, your role is to help your team find their hedgehog within the company, if possible. The author Jim Collins wrote in his book *From Good to Great*, "Get the **right people** on the **bus**, the **wrong people** off the **bus**, and the **right people** in the **right** seats." When someone is their "right seat" or wheelhouse, they can add more value to their organization and usually are happier doing it, regardless of whether they are the owner of that business. Our sole mission with this book is to share our experiences to help spark and inspire people to find their hedgehog.

Thank you for reading our book. We hope that it was both an educational and interesting read. Consider others who could benefit from this book and recommend it to them. Over the years, many people we know personally and authors we never met have inspired us through their words. We hope to do the same for others.

We would like to share some information we think will help you in your quest for finding your hedgehog. Start by writing down things that you are passionate about. This starts with you because you know what excites you. You can ask others, but this exercise really should be a personal exercise first. Take a personal assessment survey. Get to know yourself using those tools. We recommend doing a couple of different ones. Secondly, assess your skills by listing the things you do well. For this list, you may want to consider asking others for feedback. We recommend that you do a "360 feedback," essentially getting feedback from peers, direct reports (if you have any), and your leaders/managers. There is a tool called the "360 feedback," which you can find online, and there are several companies that can help you set it up to begin the process. Some of the personal survey administrators can also do a post-survey consultation to help you understand and develop a personal growth/profitability action plan. Lastly, study the market(s), industry, or career choices you have in mind. The goal is to assess whether it will be a profitable option for you. For example, some markets, industries, or careers can be more lucrative than others. While you should start with passion in determining your hedgehog, if you are passionate about an industry or career that does pay well, and the profit margins are low, you should not expect a level of monetary success beyond what that profession or industry can bring. Success is in the eyes of the beholder, but be realistic with your expectations.

Ultimately, the goal is to find the "sweet spot," which is the intersection between passion, skill, and profit. Once you find it, you will be able to add value to the world around you, your clients, customers, and your employees. When you find your hedgehog, you will be happier, more fulfilled, and more productive because you'll love what you do, and your work will stop being work.

We trust this has been helpful to you. To learn more about us and how you can continue growing, please visit our website at www.GoCriticalPath.com or follow us at https://www.facebook.com/CriticalPathConsulting/.

You can also sign up for our newsletter at our website.

To set an appointment to discuss a workshop, speaking, or coaching, send us a message through our website when you click the "Contact Us" link.

Thank you for reading our book. Now go Find Your Hedgehog and STOP Working.

About the Authors

Socrate Exantus is the CEO of four (4) All County Property Management franchise offices. Prior to joining the All County Franchise system, Socrate spent 15 years with his former employer where he held several leadership positions, with his most recent position serving as the Senior Sales Operations Manager for their National Inside Sales Division. He managed large real estate projects, sales, marketing, system integrations, training & development, and strategic planning. Socrate is currently a Real Estate Broker and Real Estate Instructor. Socrate purchased his first investment property while he was a college student at UCF. As an investor, Socrate has purchased and sold many of his own rental properties. As a CEO at All County, Socrate and his team have managed over 2,400 homes for small and institutional investors. His mission is to effectively lead his team to deliver superior property management service to every client by focusing on the Vital Signs and Key Performance Indicators of their industry. Socrate has served as the President of the All County Advisory Council and led his team to be named the "Top All County Office" in the franchise for 6 consecutive years (2011-2016). Socrate is a Leadership Speaker and regularly speaks at National Real Estate conferences and Universities (including Indiana University, and the University of Central Florida). Socrate has a Masters in Project Management from The George Washington University and a BA in Management from the University of Central Florida.

In 2019, Socrate received the Entrepreneurial Alumni Award at the University of Central Florida Hall of Fame annual Gala.

Cassandra Exantus has over 15 years of combined real estate and customer service experience. Prior to joining All County CFL, she was with Concord Management Ltd., the national leader in high quality, customer focused property management of multi-family and single family affordable rental housing communities. She served as an Assistant Community Director and managed a portfolio of five communities in East Orlando. Cassandra won several awards as top sales consultant earning over 30 Million dollars in revenue for D.R. Horton and KB Homes. Cassandra is a licensed Realtor and has worked with Prudential Real Estate and Exit Realty. She is also a member of Orlando Regional Realtor Association ORRA, National Association of Residential Property Managers –NARPM, and National Association of Realtors-NAR. Cassandra holds a BA with a focus in Advertising/Public Relations from the University of Central Florida.

Made in the USA
Monee, IL
22 June 2024